FOR THE LOVE OF BOMBS

FOR THE LOVE OF BOMBS

THE TRAIL OF NUCLEAR SUFFERING

PEDER ANKER

ANTHEM PRESS

Anthem Press
An imprint of Wimbledon Publishing Company
www.anthempress.com

This edition first published in UK and USA 2025
by ANTHEM PRESS
75–76 Blackfriars Road, London SE1 8HA, UK
or PO Box 9779, London SW19 7ZG, UK
and
244 Madison Ave #116, New York, NY 10016, USA

British Library Cataloguing-in-Publication Data
A catalogue record for this book is available from the British Library.

Library of Congress Cataloging-in-Publication Data: 2024941031
A catalog record for this book has been requested.

ISBN-13: 978-1-83999-316-9 (Pbk)
ISBN-10: 1-83999-316-2 (Pbk)

Cover Credit: Don English, Las Vegas News Bureau, LVCVA Archive

This title is also available as an e-book.

CONTENTS

THE TRAIL OF NUCLEAR SUFFERING

Farewell Oppenheimer

"The force from which the sun draws its power has been loosed against those who brought war to the Far East," announced President Harry S. Truman, hours after "the largest bomb ever yet used in the history of warfare" exploded on the city of Hiroshima on August 6, 1945.[1] Secretary of War, Henry L. Stimson, followed up with a slightly longer statement signaling out one man, the theoretical physicist J. Robert Oppenheimer, among thousands of others involved in the top-secret Manhattan Project that had led to the creation of this new weapon. "The development of the bomb itself has been largely due to his genius and the inspiration and leadership he has given to his associates," he stated.[2]

The president, his secretary of war, and his close staff were well prepared. They not only had constructed the most destructive bomb known to human-kind—they also had a winning story to tell where this terrifying weapon emerged as a force of good, one that saved rather than destroyed lives, one that could help them achieve peace rather than war, and ultimately lead to economic prosperity even if through momentary destruction. They were ready for this moment. At the core of their narrative was a report entitled *Atomic Energy for Military Purposes* prepared by the Princeton physicist Henry DeWolf Smyth, an expert in radioactive weaponry and a member of the secret S-1 Uranium

---

1 Harry S. Truman, "Statement by the President Announcing the Use of the A-Bomb at Hiroshima," *National Archives*, August 6, 1945.
2 Henry L. Stimson, "Statement of the Secretary of War," *Archive of the Atomic Heritage Foundation*, August 6, 1945.

Committee, who advised the military on how to develop the bomb.[3] Known today as the *Smyth Report*, its central message was clear: in the hands of the Americans, nuclear bombs and nuclear power were an unambiguous force of good. Most laypeople in the United States had a festive reaction to the events in Japan that reflected an end to war. The report was issued in the context of these celebrations, focusing on the intellectual achievements of the nuclear science community.

It is a truism that history is written by its winners, and the history of the making of atomic bombs is no exception. The head of the Manhattan Project General Leslie Richard Groves controlled this victorious narrative with an iron fist. He embedded the *New York Times* journalist William L. Laurence in the Manhattan Project, who would answer directly to him as the only person authorized to write about the weapon and its creation. Laurence would never raise critical questions, but followed Groves's account at every turn making, in effect, the *New York Times* into a vehicle of state propaganda, informing the public what it needed to know—nothing more and nothing else well into the 1950s. The rest of the journalists would largely follow suit.

The *Smyth Report* was at the core of Groves's propaganda campaign of sugarcoating the bomb. Working out of his office at the Princeton, Smyth was under twenty-four-hour armed guard surveillance with drafts for the report protected by army officers.[4] Groves released the text from the vault the night of August 11, 1945, and handed it over to the press for publication in the next morning's news. When it arrived in book form, it quickly became a phenomenal success with it being on the *New York Times* bestseller list from October 1945 to January 1946, selling 127,000 copies in its first eight printings. It was the only account available, and it consequently served as a "censorship guideline and classification manual" for other possible interpretations.[5]

The *Smyth Report* was a crafty account of the events meant to guide the public away from critical questioning. While the skin and hair were falling off the Japanese victims due to the exposure to radioactivity, U.S. journalists

3 Henry DeWolf Smyth under the auspices of the United States Government, *Atomic Energy for Military Purposes* (Princeton: Princeton University Press, 1945).
4 E. C. Holt and Brendan Gill, "The Talk of the Town," *The New Yorker*, January 19, 1946, 14–15.
5 Rebecca Press Schwartz, *The Making of the History of the Atomic Bomb: Henry DeWolf Smyth and the Historiography of the Manhattan Project*, Ph.D. thesis (Princeton: Department of History, Princeton University, 2008), 107.

following the narrative of the report wrote enthusiastically about the glittering scientific achievements of atomic physicists. While citizens of Hiroshima and Nagasaki were slowly dying in gruesome pain from their radioactive blisters, American citizens waived their flags celebrating the highbrow minds of nuclear science. At the core was the nation's scientific superiority and the idea that the bomb had the ability "to end all wars" (as Smyth put it).[6] In looking back on his decision to annihilate Hiroshima, President Truman would pick up this sentiment and argue that "dropping the bombs ended the war, saved lives, and gave the free nations a chance to face the facts."[7]

For all the celebration of the physicists, it is notable that Groves did not have much respect for them. He considered the scientists working in the Manhattan Project's Los Alamos Laboratory "the greatest bunch of prima donnas ever seen in one place!"[8] If the salary is an indicator of status among bomb makers, the supposed "father of the bomb" was low on the totem pole, earning a lot less than some of the other scientists Groves oversaw.[9] Yet Groves felt that Oppenheimer had something in excess of others: an overweening ambition that could serve him well. Thus began the promotion of Oppenheimer as a key figure where the physicist first became a poster child and later a scapegoat, depending on what was needed.[10] While "engineers and chemists handily outnumbered physicists" within the Manhattan Project, the physicists and Oppenheimer's work at Los Alamos on the assemblage and testing of the first bomb is still at the core of popular atomic lore.[11] Indeed, the deflection of public attention has been remarkably successful, with the narrative of the *Smyth Report* still prevailing in today's scholarly as well as popular literature about the making of the bomb. Oppenheimer has become a marker of scientific and cultural superiority.

---

6 Smyth, *Smyth Report*, 1945, 247.
7 Harry Truman in a letter to James L. Cate, January 12, 1953, *Atomic Archive*.
8 Quoted in Stephane Groueff, *Manhattan Project the Untold Story of the Making of the Atomic Bomb* (Boston: Little, Brown, 1967), 204.
9 Oppenheimer earned $10,000 a year while, in comparison, Roger Williams, the overall supervisor for DuPont, earned $26,400. Schwartz, *Making of the History*, 2008, 40.
10 Albert Berger, *Life and Times of the Bomb* (New York: Routledge, 2016), 46–49.
11 Alex Wellerstein, *Restricted Data: The History of Nuclear Secrecy in the United States* (Chicago: University of Chicago Press, 2021), 101.

Why do so many narrators continue to tell a story that scholars have determined to be not only inadequate but, in many respects, simply false?[12] So much hung on the success of the narrative of the *Smyth Report*: American moral and technical superiority, justification for the secrecy that enveloped a multi-billion project that was kept away from Congressional oversight, the payoff of research and development of science and technology, the flush funding of research universities and laboratories during an era of extreme deprivations, the segregation of black labor in production factories, the exclusion of women from sites of power, the pillaging and exploitation of planetary resources, and much more. It was to be a simple story of good versus evil with the United States, its president, cabinet, and military, squarely on one side. It was to be a solid foundation that characterized the "American" values of the 1950s and beyond. It all came together in the narration of the tortured genius of Oppenheimer.

The chief purpose of placing Oppenheimer at the core of state propaganda was to disguise everything of importance. By focusing on the petit-bourgeois neuroses of Oppenheimer and the adventures he led at the Los Alamos Laboratory, the *Smyth Report* concealed where the uranium came from and to whom it belonged. The report said little about the enrichment of uranium as that process was the true secret of nuclear weapon making. That is true even today, as in the case of uranium enrichment in the nuclear weapon program in Iran. The assembling of the bomb that took place in Los Alamos was the easy part. Indeed, how-to blueprints are today available online for the curious reader. Acquiring and enriching uranium, on the other hand, was (and still is) the real challenge. No wonder then that the *Smyth Report* kept the reader mostly in the dark about these issues while focusing on Oppenheimer.

The latest recapitulation of the *Smyth Report* has been the *Oppenheimer* film (2023) which won the Oscar for "Best Picture" in 2024. It is a familiar story of military, scientific, and technological superiority, spiced up with beautiful women, along with some political and moral hand-wringing, with first-class acting portraying brilliant and tormented physicists punching equations in their pursuit of the ultimate weapon. We even meet an aging Albert Einstein, when historical pointers back to the radiochemist Marie Curie would have been more accurate. Tellingly, the film leaves out the enrichment of uranium, not to mention the horrors that took place in Hiroshima and Nagasaki. The

---

12 Beverly Deepe Keever, *News Zero: The New York Times and the Bomb* (Monroe: Common Courage Press, 2004). Jimena Canales, "The Secret PR Push That Shaped the Atomic Bomb's Origin Story," *The Atlantic,* April 18, 2017, online.

radioactive hell at the Japanese ground zero is replaced with a Hollywood-style happy ending. As this book will show, the *Oppenheimer* film is consistent with how the U.S. popular media have portrayed the bomb in the past, including the use of (an)atomic women to sex up the bomb. Indeed, it was after seeing the film I decided to take a stand and publish this book to mobilize alternative narratives.

The narrative of the film has been fed by an army of historians writing book after book devoted to factualizing Smyth's report about all those dazzling physicists. Kai Bird and Martin J. Sherwin's *American Prometheus: The Triumph and Tragedy of J. Robert Oppenheimer* (2005) may serve as one of many examples.[13] These stories are of the tormented souls of elitist physicists who made a Faustian bargain with the military in pursuit of nuclear knowledge, while they tend to ignore the suffering and violence of the bomb to laypeople in general, and marginalized groups in particular. Readers of the Oppenheimer story are typically spared from learning about the Indigenous people who got cancers from uranium mining, for example. Not to mention the "downwinders" (as they are known) who suffered from cancers due to being exposed to the radioactive fallout from the bombs, or also all those ordinary soldiers, blue-collar workers, and people of color who got cancer.[14]

The official history of the atomic bomb in its different incarnations teaches us to forget and not to remember. As a historian of the environmental sciences and not physics, I have chosen to cast aside most of the literature about the Los Alamos scientists as someone else's embarrassment. For the love of bombs, let us say farewell to Oppenheimer.

An Atomic History from Below

"I do not believe it will bring much joy to humanity but only destruction," said Clarence R. Branch, an African American garage owner in New Jersey, about the bomb only days after the horrors in Hiroshima and Nagasaki.[15] Instead of

---

13 Kai Bird and Martin J. Sherwin, *American Prometheus: The Triumph and Tragedy of J. Robert Oppenheimer* (New York: Alfred A. Knopf, 2005). The Library of Congress Catalog lists 180 books with "Robert Oppenheimer" in the title.
14 Sarah Alisabeth Fox, *Downwind: A People's History of the Nuclear West* (Lincoln, NE: Bison Books, 2018). Trisha T. Pritikin, *The Hanford Plaintiffs: Voices from the Fight for Atomic Justice* (Lawrence, KS: University Press of Kansas, 2020).
15 Anonymous, "Atomic Bomb Brings Fear of Cave Life," *Afro-American*, August 18, 1945, 17.

repeating the state propaganda coming out of Washington, a journalist working for the African Americans would ask ordinary citizens on the street what they thought about the events. The newspaper thus captured early voices of resistance to the gruesome weapon and an alternative atomic narrative emerging from below. People on the street were scared that the bomb could bring them back to "cave life" if dropped on their community.[16]

The first resistance to the official *Smyth Report* in the United States came from these marginalized citizens on the street in the New York region, and they reacted with shock to the destructiveness of nuclear weapons. In a matter of weeks, the same African American friendly press labeled the new weapon as a "white" immoral bomb "in the eyes of the dark-skinned peoples of Asia and Africa."[17] A couple of months later, in October 1945, the black journalist Charles H. Loeb wrote his first moving report on how Hiroshima was "demolished."[18] The fine historian Vincent J. Intondi reviewed these and other early voices of opposition to the bomb in some detail, and he showed that the social movement against nuclear weapons in the United States owed its origins to African American journalists and concerned citizens. To place the beginning of the nuclear resistance within Oppenheimer's tormented soul, his leftist friends, among other Los Alamos physicists, in the Russell–Einstein Manifesto (1955), the first Pugwash Conference (1957), or amid highbrow *New York Times* intellectuals is a distortion of history. We owe the resistance to nuclear weapons in the United States to lay citizens in general and to communities of color in particular.

We also owe a great deal to the exceptional journalist John Hersey. His monumental report, *Hiroshima*, published in *The New Yorker* in August 1946 and subsequently as a book stands out as arguably the most important piece of journalism of the twentieth century.[19] Images from his report are stuck in my mind, serving as the prime motivator behind my writings in this book. I encourage everyone to read slowly Hersey's macabre tales of the nuclear

---

16 Anonymous, "17 Atomic Bombs Would Completely Destroy Boro," *New York Amsterdam News*, August 18, 1945, 15. J. A Rogers, "Atomic Bomb May Disclose That Civilized Man is Headed Back to the Caves," *The Pittsburgh Courier*, September 1, 1945, 7.

17 George Padmore, "Morals of Whites Dropped with Atom Bomb," *The Chicago Defender*, September 8, 1945, 5.

18 Charles H. Loeb, "Loeb Reflects On Atomic Bombed Area," *Atlanta Daily World*, October 5, 1945, 1. Vincent J. Intondi, *African Americans against the Bomb* (Stanford: Stanford University Press, 2015), 9–28.

19 John Hersey, *Hiroshima* (New York: Alfred Knopf, 1946). Lesley M. M. Blume, *Fallout: The Hiroshima Cover-up and the Reporter who Revealed It to the World* (New York: Simon & Schuster, 2020).

theater of cruelty. Indeed, if you have not read it, stop reading my book now and begin with his. I still shiver from reading the stories of Hatsuyo Nakamura, Terufumi Sasaki, Wilhelm Kleinsorge, Toshiko Sasaki, Masakazu Fujii, Kiyoshi Tanimoto, Toshio Nakamura, and others directly impacted by the bomb. As will be pointed out, the larger mobilization against these weapons outside the United States belongs to Japanese activism after the Castle Bravo detonation and destruction of the Bikini Atoll in 1954.

Taking the cue from Hersey, this book will pursue what is known as the "people's history" approach to the bomb by focusing on the importance of the lives of ordinary and marginalized citizens. Consequently, the archival material and evidence are almost exclusively from popular newspapers, lowbrow magazines, and other outlets and books reflecting the life of commoners. All histories are reflections on current affairs, and that includes this book. The emerging literature on the people's history of atomic bombs points to an alternative and more truthful story of resistance that may—hopefully—inspire readers to mobilize politically against this horrific weapon. In reading the stories of the victims, and by beginning to dismantle the official history of the atomic bomb, I hope to open up the possibility of examining the controversial thesis that nothing good came from the bomb. Not even victory.

President Truman's argument that the bomb "ended the war" and saved lives is simply not true. Some of his closest military advisers, such as Admiral William D. Leahy, argued to the contrary: "the use of this barbarous weapon at Hiroshima and Nagasaki was of no material assistance in our war against Japan. The Japanese were already defeated and ready to surrender because of the effective sea blockade and the successful bombing with conventional weapons."[20] Similarly, General Dwight D. Eisenhower held that "Japan was already defeated and that dropping the bomb was completely unnecessary."[21] Yet the belief that the bombs somehow ended the war would prevail in the larger public thanks to the White House's careful handling of public relations. Consider the top-secret memo from General George Lincoln to Eisenhower from April 1946 that stresses the importance of guiding the public so that ordinary people would not realize that victory was secured before the bombs were dropped. "The implication that the atomic bombs were dropped on a people

20 William D. Leahy, *I was There* (London: Victor Gollancz, 1950), 513–514.
21 Dwight D. Eisenhower, *Mandate for Change* (New York: Doubleday, 1963), 313.

who had already sued for peace should not be included in a paper prepared for release to the public."[22]

President Truman's administration also did its best to play down the gruesome suffering from radioactive poisoning the citizens in Japan underwent. At stake was not only the production of more bombs but also the possibility peaceful use of atomic energy. A series of public hearings were to shed light on the matter in the fall of 1945. General Groves was called to testify to the U.S. Senate about the possible hazards of radioactive materials, and he played down its dangers by reassuring the Senators. Those few killed by radioactive fallout, he stated, had found it to be "a very pleasant way to die."[23]

There are numerous films, documentaries, autobiographical accounts, articles, and books providing evidence to the contrary about the *coventration* (a military term for the complete annihilation of a city through firebombing). Yet it would be a mistake to think of the bomb as only being destructive to the poor citizens of Hiroshima and Nagasaki, along with the downwinders in the United States and the Pacific. It was also nefarious to the American environment, politics, culture, and science. The bomb's environmental history was caustic from the initial mining of uranium to their explosions in what became ecological sacrifice zones and disaster sites in the Pacific and Nevada. (Why is it that historians and bomb makers alike still call them "test sites"?) The bomb was destructive to the political sphere's ability to discuss military matters. It was caustic to popular culture from drinking alcohol (as in getting "bombed") to erotic complementation (as in being called a "sex bomb"). The bomb was damaging to the scientific cultures that produced the bomb. It has even been destructive to the way historians cast the history of the bomb in all too apologetic terms. Nothing good came from the bomb. Nothing.

Consequently, this book does not begin with some convoluted equations on the blackboard in a highbrow laboratory but in a dirty mine in the Dene First Nation in northern Canada. It was here the uranium began its path of pain. It was dug up by blue-collar miners and handled by Indigenous people with their bare hands. Their work and suffering from subsequent cancers represent the origin of the trail of nuclear suffering that the bomb created. The

22 George Lincoln to Dwight D. Eisenhower, April 2. 1946. Quoted in Gar Alperovitz, *The Decision to Use the Atomic Bomb* (New York: Knopf, 1995), 626.
23 Leslie R. Groves testimony to the U.S. Senate Special Committee on Atomic Energy, November 30, 1945, quoted in Patrick B. Sharp, *Savage Perils: Racial Frontiers and Nuclear Apocalypse in American Culture* (Norman: University of Oklahoma Press, 2007), 133.

first warnings against the destructive impact of the bomb did not come from some highbrow thinker, but from dark indigenous prophesies of the 1880s, long before anyone imagined the destructive power of uranium. As handlers of uranium, their story is the first chapter in a people's history of the making of the bomb. It is a tale of settler colonialism, exploitation, and death due to cancers from being exposed to nuclear materials. The Dene people's suffering represents the beginning of the path of pain that would follow nuclear materials to Japan, to disaster sites on Pacific atolls, and ultimately to the catacombs with nuclear waste.

The uranium from Canada would first end up in the ultra-secret town of Wheat in Tennessee, or what was left of it, as the village was (except for their church) erased by military authorities. On their land, radiochemists began working on the complicated process of uranium enrichment. The K-25 factory enriching the uranium for the Manhattan Project blew up the social and moral fabric of Wheat's communal living with the land. The destructiveness of nuclear bombs was thus not only in their explosive power but also in the environmental impact on the land they were produced. The destruction of the Wheat community also entailed a new social order of atomic individualism realized in the post-war town of Oak Ridge, which was built on the ruins of Wheat. It became a model town for the nation, all of which will be the topic of the second chapter.

The point of departure of the third chapter is the immense joy U.S. citizens felt for having annihilated the cities of Hiroshima and Nagasaki. The many analogies between nuclear weapons and a woman's body emerged in the context of these celebrations, which also included alcoholic bombs and mushroom-shaped chocolate cakes. Describing a woman as "a sex bomb" or "a bombshell" has since become part of daily (college) language. In this imagery, the female is destructive in her immense attraction, whereas the male is the victim of her overpowering beauty. In the aftermath of Hiroshima, being compared to nuclear bombs became an analogy for romance, compliments, and sexual fantasies. Newspaper cuttings and commentaries in popular magazines portray female bodies in the language of nuclear weaponry, with their sexiness helping to tame and doll up the portrayal of gruesome bombs in the public imagination.

The bikini outfit worn by nuclear "bombshells" was named after the Bikini Atoll, and the U.S. colonial policies in the Pacific will be the topic of the fourth chapter. It is a history of nuclear bombing that shattered islands and their people. How islanders reacted to the bombing and the ignorance and violence by the colonizers who made their ocean the dumping ground for radioactive waste serve as this book's colonial history.

The last chapter turns to the sky and post-war explanations for why the climate was getting warmer. Newspapers and popular magazines covered increasing temperatures in North America in this period, and laypeople blamed nuclear bombing for heating the atmosphere. This allowed scientists to introduce emissions of carbon dioxide from the burning of fossil fuels as an alternative explanation for global warming. In this way, the citizen's voice became of key importance in establishing the possibility of anthropogenic climate change. Although incorrect about the warming power of nuclear explosions for the climate, the voice of the public created an acceptance of the idea that humans could be the cause of global temperature increases.

CHAPTER 1

AT THE END OF THE WORLD

Sombe Ke, "The Money Place"

About 150 years ago, in the 1880s, a medicine man of the Dene First Nation made a chilling prophecy. Ehtseo (grandfather) Louis Ayah (1857–1940) was still young, but would soon become their recognized spiritual leader. He was hunting with some friends for caribou along the eastern shore of the Sahtú (the Great Bear Lake). They had ignored traditional beliefs and camped for the night by some large rocky cliffs known as Sombe Ke ("the money place"). A forbidden site, those cliffs were said to be bad for health if anyone stayed in their proximity. In the middle of the night, Ayah awoke suddenly and began singing until the very morning. When he was done, his fellow hunters asked him what was going on. "I foresaw many things and I was disturbed," he told them. He continued:

> I saw people going into a big hole in the ground—strange people, not Dene. Their skin was white. They were going into a hole with all kinds of metal tools and machines and making a lot of noise, so I followed them. They were going back and forth into that hole. They were digging a great tunnel. [...] On the surface where they lived, there were strange houses with smoke coming out of them. Another thing I saw were [sic] big boats with smoke coming out of them, going back and forth on the river. And I saw a flying bird—a big one. They were loading it with things. It didn't seem to harm anybody, but it made a lot of noise. [...] I watched them and finally saw what they were making with whatever they were digging out of the hole—it was something long, like a stick. I wanted to know what it was for—I saw what harm it would do when the big bird dropped this thing on people— they all died from this long stick, which burned everyone. [...] The people they dropped this long thing on looked like us, like Dene. I wondered if this would happen on our land or if it would harm our people. But I saw no one

FOR THE LOVE OF BOMBS

harmed here, only the material that was taken out of our land by people who were just living among us. That bothered me. But it isn't for now; it's a long time in the future. It will come after we are all dead.[1]

The prophecy has been haunting the Sahtu Got'ine (Dene-speaking people who live around Great Bear Lake) ever since, passed down from generation to generation, deciphered and emulated. At first, they did not know what to make of it. Looking back at it today, most of them think that it came true. The rocky cliffs where the prophecy was given became the site for the mine that delivered the majority of the uranium for the Manhattan Project. Perhaps the "stick" resembled the elongated shape of nuclear bombs, and the people who were burned were the citizens of Hiroshima? Why did the hunters choose to rest by the forbidden cliffs? And could it all have been avoided, had they listened more carefully to the prophecy? These are questions the Sahtu Got'ine have been struggling with since then. The dark prophecy represents the first murmurings of a history that begins far away from where histories of nuclear bombs usually launch. Instead of starting with the work of anguished physicists, the history of nuclear weaponry may as well begin at the material origin of bomb-making and with the labor that made it possible at Sombe Ke, "the money place."

The mine at Sombe Ke is located at Cameron Bay, an inlet along the eastern shoreline of the Great Bear Lake, near the Arctic Circle in the Dene First Nation. As long as anyone can recall, the Sahtu Got'ine have been living peacefully as nomadic people in coexistence with the Sahtú. "The Dene were at one with the land, knowing how to live in every season, in every place. [...] They knew their land so well that, as they journeyed through their vast territory, they were never lost," a knower of their culture, Sara Stewart, notes.[2] When not traveling to hunt and fish, they lived in the Déline village, which means "where the waters flow," referring to the path of water from the lake into the Sahtúdé (Great Bear River). Selling or trading animal skins was a chief source of income, which left a paper trail with the North West Company

1 Louis Ayah quoted in George Blondin, *When the World was New* (Yellowknife: Outcrop, The Northern Publishers, 1990), 78–79.
2 Sarah Stewart, "Sidebar," in *Remember: The Coming of the White Man* (Calgary, Alberta: Durvile Books, 2021), 206.

beginning in 1799. This paper trail allows them to enter Western versions of history in the form of parcels of fur and written documents.[3]

By 1930, when the mine at Sombe Ke opened, the historical significance of the Sahtu Got'ine in colonial accounts would still be measured in terms of goods, except that the type of commodity had changed. Still nameless, they now emerge in mining records in terms of how many sacks of mineral ore they could carry.[4] They carried bags of it from the mine to a waiting boat which would ship it out for further processing. It was tedious work that lasted all day and sometimes extended into the night. To make matters worse, the bags were heavy, 110 lbs. (50 kg), and they had no way to carry them except on their shoulders. It could take five to six days to fill the boat, after which they were allowed a rest. At times, the bags, made of cotton or jute, would spill, so they would have to gather the spilled mineral with their bare hands as best as they could, and place it in a new bag. In the course of this work, it was hard, almost impossible, to not inhale the dusty powder.

The workers' families lived on the other side of Sahtú in the Délįne village. This was also the home of Ayah, who made a series of dark predictions in the 1930s. He spoke of the changing lifestyle of Dene culture, which was under pressure from Canadian colonialism and modernization, such as mining. Among his many gloomy forewarnings, Ayah predicted that the Sahtu Got'ine would suffer from a "new kind of sickness you have never heard of" and that there would also be "horrible things you have never seen before."[5] These prophecies were barely audible or discussed, even among Indigenous people. Today, the Sahtu Got'ine believe these predictions came true, as within the next decades, Délįne villagers were hit by rare cancers of the neck and shoulders, the same areas where they had carried the bags of ore.

---

3 Michael Asch, "The Dene Economy," in *Dene Nation – The Colony Within*, ed. Mel Watkins (Toronto: University of Toronto Press, 1977), 47–46.

4 The archives of the Eldorado Mine are not accessible to the public due to nuclear secrecy, with the exception of Robert Bothwell's helpful and detailed history *Eldorado: Canada's National Uranium Company* (Toronto: University of Toronto Press, 1984), with labor culture discussed on pages 38–77.

5 Louis Ayah, "The Prophecy's of Louis Ayah," *The People*, 2016. Undated 1930s, or earlier.

The Eldorado Gold Mine

The colonial history of uranium mining starts with the prospector Gilbert
LaBine (1890–1977), who, in 1926, was a recent graduate of the Haileybury
Provincial School of Mines, in the town of Cobalt (Ontario). The unearthing
of silver in Cobalt in 1903 resulted in a silver rush to the town and the opening of the largest silver mining camp in the world, with the new riches making
the School of Mines the best and most prominent mining school in Canada.
LaBine was amid this silver craze, observing firsthand how wealth could fall
quickly into the hands of prospectors. He did some of it himself in the Cobalt
region and founded The Eldorado Gold Mines Ltd., in 1926, to pursue the
cause. There were numerous prospectors around Cobalt, and some of them
were indeed successful. The name of his company was designed to lure investors into financing his search for treasures. Enthused by the possibility of finding silver and gold, he studied the Geological Survey of Canada and various
explorer accounts of possible mineral ores along the eastern shore of the Great
Bear Lake.

In 1930, LaBine went to explore the area himself and met a Sahtu Got'ine
known as Old Beyonnie, who showed him a rock with interesting minerals
he had found at Sombe Ke. Noticing that it was pitchblende (or *uraninite*, in
today's terminology), he gave Beyonnie $20 for the mining rights along with
a verbal promise of a percentage of the profit (which never materialized) and
subsequently registered the mining rights for Sombe Ke region under his company's name.[6] To LaBine, the place was simply unexplored land that could—
and should—be developed to generate wealth for the nation, and himself. This
type of settler colonialism involves, as Traci Brynne Voyles has pointed out,
a "complex construction of that land as either always belonging to the settler—his manifest destiny—or as undesirable, unproductive, or unappealing,
in short as wasteland."[7] The eastern shore of the Great Bear Lake was indeed
perceived as unproductive land to be exploited by LaBine, and the irony here
is that the land actually became an unproductive polluted wasteland, or what

6 Joe Blondin, "Uranium," in *We Remember: The Coming of the White Man* (Calgary, Alberta:
Durvile Books, 2021), 204; Bothwell, *Eldorado*, 1984, 20–23.
7 Traci Brynne Voyles, *Wastelanding: Legacies of Uranium Mining in Navajo Country*
(Minneapolis: University of Minnesota Press, 2015), 7. Max Liboiron, *Pollution is
Colonialism* (Durham: Duke University Press, 2021).

Marco Armiero calls a "wasteocene" because of the mining of radioactive materials LaBine initiated.[8]

Pitchblende is the uranium-rich radioactive material from which Marie and Pierre Curie extracted the radium chloride compound back in 1898. By 1911, they had further isolated the radium chloride to its metallic state. Radium was used for experimental and medical purposes, most prominently as a promising component in a cure for cancer. Its ability to glow in the dark made the metal alluring to the general public as well, where it was used in state-of-the-art watches and high-end toys for children. Its many uses made radium a true societal gem. The newly discovered metal became, in the words of the historian of science Luis Campos, "the secret of life."[9] A 1913 article from the *New York Times*, for example, reported that with the discovery of radium, "Science [was] on Road to Revolutionize all Existence." The "march of science" would, thanks to radium, liberate new powerful energy for human use and the "Results Would Be Vast" as "an ounce of radium would produce as much effect as much as many tons of the most powerful detonator known."[10]

Radium was new and novel. It represented the cutting edge of scientific research, and the virtues of the metal were to lead to human prosperity and progress. No wonder then that in the mid-1920s it became the most luxurious and expensive metal in the world, with a price tag of over $100,000 a gram. That would not last long, with the discovery of a rich ore in the Belgian Congo. The Belgians (or the poor African Congolese miners working for the Belgians) would drive out their competitors with inexpensive radium, in effect creating a world monopoly on its production by 1930. Yet it was still a lucrative business, fetching $75,000 a gram (or about $1.4 million a gram in today's money).[11]

It was the possibility of earning money on radium that lay behind LaBine's decision to open a mine at Sombe Ke in 1930 under his company name the Eldorado Gold Mine. Owning shares in the mine represented an investment in the future, and LaBine used the novelty of radium and its high monetary value to promote his company. In the late 1920s, there were speculations in the press and among scientists on the possible transmutation of radioactive metals

8 Marco Armiero, *Wasteocene: Stories from the Global Dump* (Cambridge: Cambridge University Press, 2021).

9 Luis Campos, *Radium: The Secret of Life* (Chicago: University of Chicago Press, 2015).

10 Frederick Soddy, "Science on Road to Revolutionize all Existence," *New York Times*, September 28, 1913, SM6.

11 Bothwell, *Eldorado*, 1984, 7–8.

into gold. This ultimate alchemical dream would even cause worries within the official U.S. federal government about a monetary collapse if scientists succeeded in making gold.[12] Yet, by 1932, the Eldorado Mine would take "gold" out of its name as it became clear that pitchblende for the purpose of extracting highly valued radium would be the mine's sole purpose. The ore at Cameron Bay was considered to be rich in comparison to its chief competitor in the Belgian Congo. In Eldorado, it took 15 tons of ore to recover 1 gram of radium, although the process was cumbersome and, in the end, barely profitable. The mine would extract about 1 ton of ore a day and ship it out for processing. Soon, Sombe Ke was renamed Port Radium, complete with a settlement in the proximity of the mines where the workers could rest.

The workers within the mine were mostly immigrants of European descent, as the tooling required special skills and social trust, whereas Indigenous people carried the bags of uranium ore from the mine to the dock from where M/S Radio Gilbert (named after Gilbert LaBine) would transport it away for further processing. The Eldorado Mine was built with a colonialist ethic of conquering foreign land and its people for the benefit of white settlers. It was a racist mindset and sense of superiority that allowed its culture of exploitation. It was all driven by visions of radium as a bringer of prosperity and progress.

This had consequences for how Eldorado would run its mine. The initial expenses in opening a mine were massive, but they were an acceptable risk considering radium represented the very future of humankind. While waiting for the profit to materialize, the miners were given salaries well below comparable occupational wages in the region. As it turned out, the prospect of progress would keep their compensations below living wage for decades, as the mine would not earn enough to pay the shareholders any dividend or raise the miners' compensations until after the war. The hope for prosperity was what kept both investors and blue-collar workers going.

The belief in progress also had consequences for the handling of pitchblende. Because radium was regarded as an intrinsically good thing, only true skeptics would question its many virtues. The exception to this trend was an engineer within the Canadian government's Department of Mines who spoke out; his name was W. R. McClelland. In a report from 1931, he wrote that

---

12 Alberto A. Matínez, *Science Secrets: The Truth about Darwin's Finches, Einstein's Wife, and Other Myths* (Puttsburgh: University of Pittsburgh Press, 2011), 91.

[r]ecent investigations in the field of radium poisoning have led to the conclusion that precautions are necessary even in the handling of substances of low radioactivity. The ingestion of small amounts of radioactive dust over a long period of time will cause a building up of radioactive material in the body, which eventually may have serious consequences. Lung cancer, bone necrosis, and rapid anemia are possible diseases due to the deposition of radioactive substances in the cell tissue or bone structure of the body.[13]

Yet, there is no evidence of his warnings being known to anyone near Eldorado, or anywhere else for that matter. Indeed, his finding seems to have been intentionally or accidentally buried, as it did not surface until recently when historians and activists began researching how much the government and the mining company knew about the dangers of radioactive material in the 1930s.[14]

None of the workers were told that being in contact with radioactive material could be dangerous. As a consequence, they did not use protective clothing and handled bags of pitchblende with their bare hands until as late as 1937. The exception to the rule was the expert in radium processing, Marcel Pochon, who negotiated a clause in his contract of continuing pay in case of radium poisoning.[15] He was aware of the dangers, although there was no evidence of him passing on the knowledge. There was not any evident ill intent from him or anyone else here. Instead, both experts and lay miners seemed to be blinded by the dream of having found a financial Eldorado.

Yet, for all their optimism, the mine did not do well financially, as it was soon caught in the downward spiral of the economic depression of the 1930s. The Belgians would ratchet up their production in Congo and saturate the market with cheap radium, causing the price to drop to $25,000 a gram by the late 1930s. Cuts in government medical spending would lead to less demand for radium, and by the summer of 1940, Eldorado was sealed, leaving only a

---

13 W. R. McClelland, "Precautions for Workers in the Treating of Radium Ores," in *Investigations in Ore Dressing and Metallurgy* (Ottawa: Department of Mines, 1931), 23. Alana J. Fletcher, "Re/mediation: The Story of Port Radium," PhD diss., Queen's University Kingston, Ontario, Canada, 2015.

14 Gordon Edwards, "Radioactivity Is Invisible but Do the Facts Have to Be Hidden as Well?" Underground Exploration Program of the Matoush Property, Mistissini, Quebec, 2010; "Uranium in Quebec: Truth and Consequences," Canadian Coalition for Nuclear Responsibility, Hampstead, Quebec, 2016.

15 Bothwell, *Eldorado*, 1984, 57. Norman Moss, *The Politics of Uranium* (London: Andre Deutsch, 1981).

couple of caretakers to keep an eye on the mine and its equipment. This would not hinder the mine's President LaBine from promoting the company's shares to raise money. As its largest shareholder, he could not let go of the social and scientific optimism concerning what radium could do.

Mining Uranium for the Manhattan Project

One of the waste products from the Eldorado Mine was lots of uranium oxide, along with some noxious arsenate, cobalt, and silver. The problem with the uranium, however, was that it had limited use. In the late 1930s, Eldorado had tried to develop a market for particularly tough uranium-grade ceramics, but it failed. They also tried to develop a market for uranium-enhanced red and orange colors for artists, with little success. They had a small market among laboratory researchers, as in the case of the National Research Council in Ottawa and Columbia University in New York, each of which purchased tiny amounts. But that was about the extent of the available market. As a result, a large amount of uranium oxide was stored at the mine, at the factory site in Port Hope, or simply dumped in nearby environments, including the Great Bear Lake.

However, the limited market and use would expand with the onslaught of the Second World War, which Canada entered in September 1939 along with the British. How could the nation contribute to the war besides sending soldiers to fight the Germans? As a country with large amounts of natural resources, the government aligned its minerals and metals for the production of weapons. Perhaps radium, with all its virtues, could also be of military interest for bomb-making? "If radium can be made a decisive factor in war," a journalist from the *Toronto Daily Star* noted in 1940, then "Germany will be out of luck for Canada has in the Eldorado mine in Great Bear Lake the largest deposit of radium in the world."[16] The board at the Eldorado Mine had worked under the assumption that they were producing a medical product, and their know-how was based on the science of geology, chemistry, and metallurgy. Now they began pondering if radium could be of any help in the war effort.

To the extent they had contact with scientific communities, it was through small shipments for laboratory work in radiochemistry. They had very little knowledge of or interest in physics. The headlines in the summer of 1939

---

16 W. R. Plewman, "The War Reviewed," *Toronto Daily Star*, February 16, 1940, 7.

FIGURE 1: The Eldorado Mine at Port Radium in 1947. ©NWT Archives/Robert van't Hoff/N-1995-007: 0022. Photo: Signalman Robert van't Hoff.

proclaimed that one "might blow world sky-high by splitting uranium atom."[17] If the scientists were able to control the energy of Uranium-235, LaBine told the press in the spring of 1940, Eldorado had accumulated large stocks of the uranium oxide to meet a "terrific overnight demand" for it.[18] On December 7, 1941, the Japanese attacked Pearl Harbor and the Americans joined the war. Only months later, in March 1942, the head of the Manhattan Project, Vannevar Bush, sent Eldorado a surprise order for 60 tons of uranium oxide. Moreover, he indicated that new and larger orders were on its way. This was truly exciting for LaBine, who quickly organized the shipment of the uranium they had stored at their sites and sent orders for his workers to begin gathering the uranium oxide they had dumped in nearby environments. These actions represent the very origin of nuclear bombs, a weapon only thinkable without plenty of uranium oxide.

17 Anonymous, "Might Blow World Sky-high by Splitting Uranium Atom," *Toronto Star*, June 19, 1939, 1, 5.
18 Anonymous, "U-235 Good as Super-Man but Miracles are Costly," *Toronto Star*, May 7, 1940, 2.

The order was large enough to reopen the Eldorado Mine. The Brits were also advancing plans to build nuclear bombs under the code name Tube Alloys and consequently ordered 20 tons of uranium dioxide from LaBine in July 1942. Given the previous large U.S. order, the Eldorado Mine could not begin working on the British order until October with eventual delivery in the summer of 1943. In the meantime, the Americans put in orders for uranium dioxide of a magnitude so large that the Brits would not get any more of it during the war.

The people at the Eldorado Mine had no clue what all the uranium was good for. There were few workers at the mine with long-term experience, as those with the know-how had moved on to other jobs when the mine closed back in the summer of 1940. As a result, the mine had to scramble to hire whoever they could convince to work for them, including high-school students, newly released jail inmates, army rejects, and women. It is the work of these unknown hands that begins the material trail—"the highway of the atom"— that led to nuclear destruction.[19] And yet there is little evidence of people being concerned about working with radioactive materials or being aware that it was for serious bomb-making. The pay was low, lower than local sanitary workers, and physically hard and monotonous. And the turnover was high. As a result, there would be accidents, inefficiencies, and miners leaving for better jobs elsewhere. Things got better when the mine got unionized in 1943, with work hours dropping from 54 to 48 hours a week. Still, Eldorado was not an attractive place to be.

Between 1942 and 1946 the Eldorado Mine would process about 2,000 tons of uranium dioxide for the Manhattan Project. It was not the only source of uranium for the Americans. Some of their uranium oxide came from the above-mentioned mine in the Belgian Congo, which had stored some of it in a warehouse in New Jersey where it was confiscated by U.S. authorities to the benefit of the war effort.[20] Another portion, about 15 percent of the uranium used for the Manhattan Project, came from piles of vanadium tailings in mines on or near the Navajo Nation in the United States.[21] Thus, the American bomb-makers relied almost exclusively on Canadian uranium oxide. The

19 Peter C. van Wyck, *The Highway of the Atom* (Montreal: McGill-Queen's University Press, 2010).
20 Vincent J. Jones, *Manhattan: The Army and the Atom Bomb* (Washington, DC: Center of Military History, 1985), 64–65.
21 Voyles, *Wastelanding*, 2.

Canadian government realized that the Eldorado mine was important for the war effort, but also of national diplomatic interest. To gain full control of the ore, the Canadian government purchased the Eldorado Mine, which provided key shareholders, including LaBine, with a healthy profit. Those, however, who had invested in the mine during the radium craze of the early 1930s, lost money. The takeover allowed the Canadian government to make sure the oxide would only be delivered to military projects, which, in effect, made the Manhattan Project the mine's only customer. The reason for the government takeover was a well-guarded military secret. The story leaked to the press stated that the government had taken over the mine because radium was of military interest, whereas the press did not mention uranium at all.[22] At the same time, Canadians initiated their wartime uranium research which helped establish a legacy of nuclear power in the nation.[23]

A Cold War Eldorado

On August 6, 1945, the bomb made with uranium oxide excavated in Eldorado exploded over Hiroshima: "We have won the battle of the laboratories" against the Germans, reported the *Toronto Star* (echoing President Truman's statement), with Canada "providing indispensable raw material" for the bomb.[24] Yet, at the end of the war, the Eldorado Mines' financial prospects were somewhat bleak. While they had a near monopoly over uranium during the war, the price of uranium was set artificially low by the Canadians as part of the country's war effort. After the war, new mines producing uranium at a lower cost soon emerged. The Belgian mine in the Congo produced oxide at about $5,000 per ton, compared to $25,000 per ton for Canadian ore. Choosing a provider was a political as well as a financial question for the Americans, who diversified their sources and financially favored uranium from the Congo.[25]

---

22 Anonymous, "Radium Mine Expropriated for 'Secret' Reason," *Toronto Daily Star*, January 29, 1944, 2.

23 Stephen A. Andrews, Madison T. Andrews, and Thomas E. Mason, "Canadian Contributions to the Manhattan Project and Early Nuclear Research," *Nuclear Technology* 207 (2021), Sup., 134–146.

24 Anonymous, "We have Won the Battle of the Laboratories," *Toronto Daily Star*, August 7, 1945, 4. Harry S. Truman, "Statement by the President Announcing the Use of the A-Bomb at Hiroshima," *National Archives*, August 6, 1945..

25 Gabrielle Hecht, *Being Nuclear: Africans and the Global Uranium Trade* (Cambridge: MIT Press, 2012).

With the production of nuclear bombs escalating during the Cold War, pitchblende became a much sought-after and diplomatically sensitive mineral oxide. At the time, the Americans were uneasy about the position of the Canadians. There were security issues with a Canadian spy ring delivering secrets to the Soviets, the issue of a political bias toward the British with Canada being part of the Commonwealth, and a general feeling of not being in direct control of material of vital importance for American interests.[26] In trying to negotiate their position, the Canadians sought to hammer out a policy for uranium oxide distribution through the United Nations, a position that made perfect sense to the Americans as long as no uranium oxide was delivered to the Soviets. To keep control of the uranium, the Americans continued to order pitchblende from Eldorado. With numerous nuclear bombs detonated in military research and the radical build-up of the nuclear arsenal, Eldorado saw a steady increase in orders. By 1950, "uranium mining and selling ha[d] become a big and profitable business," a financial journalist noted, providing Ottawa with a healthy profit.[27] New mines, including one in Saskatchewan, would provide a steady supply for the high demand. Indeed, by 1959, there were 23 uranium ore mines in Canada, valued at $330 million a year, more than any other mineral shipped out of the nation.[28]

However, the profit did not trickle down to the Sahtu Got'ine, who would continue to work 12 hours a day, six days a week for four months a year. They would sleep in Port Radium on used oxide bags and eat fish caught in contaminated water. The pattern of bodily protection had improved somewhat, with them now using gloves, although they would still breathe in the dusty powder from the bags. Unlike the white workers in the mine, the Sahtu Got'ine workers were not offered a shower so that they could wash the dust off. Back in Déline, their traditional tents were sewed together from used uranium sacks donated in

26 Amy Knight, *How the Cold War Began: The Igor Gouzenko Affair and the Hunt for Soviet Spies* (Toronto: McClelland & Stewart, 2005).

27 Hal Greer, "Eldorado Mine Gives Ottawa Neat Profit in Sale of Uranium," *Toronto Star*, July 9, 1951, 13.

28 Jim Harding, *Canada's Deadly Secret: Saskatchewan Uranium and the Global Nuclear System* (Halifax: Fernwood Pub., 2007). Bethany Haalboom, "Pursuing Openings and Navigating Closures for Aboriginal Knowledges in Environmental Governance of Uranium Mining, Saskatchewan, Canada," *The Extractive Industries and Society* 3 (2016), 1010–1017. Arn Keeling, "'Born in an Atomic Test Tube': Landscapes of Cyclonic Development at Uranium City, Saskatchewan," *The Canadian Geographer* 54:2 (2010), 228–252.

a gesture of goodwill from Eldorado. A reasonable connection between cancer and radioactive material was still questioned in local news as late as 1975.[29]

The mining would continue at Eldorado until the quality of the uranium declined and the ore was exhausted. The company also brought in machinery to dig up whatever uranium was left in the lake where it had been dumped in the 1930s. In 1960, the mine was closed, except for a short period in the 1970s when a different company extracted silver and copper at the Eldorado site. In 1982, the mine was closed for good, and Port Radium burned.

Prophecies Coming True

In 1998, the Canadian filmmaker Peter Blow released *A Village of Widows*, a moving documentary about what happened to the Délı̨ne community due to its exposure to radioactive materials.[30] It was an eye-opening film for many Canadians, made largely based on materials gathered by and interviews done with members of the Délı̨ne Uranium Committee. Among the interviewed was a committee of Sahtu Got'ine ready to address what they saw as deep environmental injustices that had been inflicted upon their people, especially on the Délı̨ne village. "In my mind it's a war crime that has been well hidden," its chairwoman Cindy Gilday said. "The Dene were the first civilian victims of the war and the last to be addressed."[31] Their chief Raymond Tutcho was equally upset: "We the Dene have been subjected to over 60 years of horrible injustice because of apparent national interests. Our people have paid for this with our lives and the health of our community, lands and waters."[32] They used

---

29 Paul Dalby, "Man says CBC Wrong to Suggest Radiation Killed Wife, Children," *Toronto Star*, August 15, 1975, A5.

30 Peter Blow, *The Village of Widows* (Ontario: Lindum Films, 1998). Déline Dene Band Council, *They Never Told Us These Things: A Record and Analysis of the Deadly and Continuing Impacts of Radium and Uranium Mining on the Sahtu Dene of Great Bear Lake, Northwest Territories, Canada* (Déline: Déline First Nation, 1998). Julie Salverson, "They Never Told Us These Things," *Maisonneuve*, August 12, 2011, Ronald B. Barbour, "Déline Dene Mining Tragedy," *First Nations Drum*, December 22, 1998.

31 Quoted in Andrew Nikiforuk, "Echoes of the Atomic Age," *Calgary Herald*, March 14, 1998, A1, A4.

32 Raymond Tutcho quoted in Dene Uranium Committee, "The Dene People of Great Bear Lake call for Federal Response to Uranium Deaths" (press release), *Arctic Circle*, March 25, 1998.

the documentary to call for an environmental clean-up of the Eldorado site and monetary compensation for lives lost.

The Village of Widows tells the story of how a community that had never registered cancer before its members died of the disease. The vast majority of the miners were men, which left the women as widows but also endangered the aspects of Dene culture that had traditionally been passed from men to their male descendants. As a result: "The Dene of Deline are now [in 1998] living in fear of their land, water, animals and worried for their own health and survival."[33] The documentary showed to all what Sahtu Got'ine had known for long, namely that Ayah's old medical prophecies about sicknesses and the destructive weapon had come true. As a result, they pleaded for environmental justice and traveled to Japan to express remorse for unknowingly having been involved in producing such a terrible weapon.[34]

Meanwhile, people in the Déline village began the process of documenting their history and the environmental injustices done. They found that out of 35 men who worked in the mine, "at least 10 have died of rare bone cancers, as well as lung, kidney, stomach, and bowel cancers—all cancers that can be caused by ionizing radiation." These were only the deaths that could be medically documented, as additional known cases of mining-related illnesses leading to death could only be confirmed by oral history. Moreover, families of those who had carried uranium oxide or people living along its transport route were subject to a high level of cancer mortality. "Women's descriptions of life and work in this economy reveal that miscarriages were common, and provide accounts of still-births and strange deaths and illnesses (like deformities and leg cancer) suffered by young children."[35] As Anna Stanley and others have shown, the emotional and physical impact of the mining on the Sahtu Got'ine has been significant.[36]

33 Cindy Kenny-Gilday, "A Village of Widows," *Arctic Circle*, [undated, probably March 1998].
34 Peter Goodspeed, "Village of Widows," *Toronto Star*, July 26, 1998, F1, F7. Danielle Knight, "Native Americans Denounce Toxic Legacy," *Third World News Agency*, 1999. Marie Clements, *Burning Vision* (Vancouver: Talon, 2003). Helen Gilbert, "Indigeneity, Time and the Cosmopolitics of Postcolonial Belonging," *Interventions* 15:2 (2013), 195–210.
35 Deline Uranium Team, *If Only We Had Known: The History of Port Radium as Told by the Sahtuotine* (Deline Uranium Team and Deline First Nation, North West Territories, 2005), 56, 92, 95, 105.
36 Anna Stanley, "Wasted Life: Labour, Liveliness, and the Production of Value," *Antipode* 47 (2015), 792–811. doi: 10.1111/anti.12128. Anna Stanley, "Natures of Risk: Capital,

The response from the Canadian government health officials to these reports has been in line with the legacy associated with the uranium mining of the 1930s. In 2005, the Canadian government scientists investigated the claims of environmental harm and concluded in its official report that the miners had not been overexposed to radiation and that the Eldorado site was "below risk levels for background exposure." They "concluded that exposure to metals on the Port Radium site will not result in adverse effects to anyone." According to the scientists, living and working in proximity to the Eldorado mine would not result in greater risk than in other places.[37] Mathematical risk modeling was behind the argument, which suggested that the unusual cancer pattern among the Sahtu Got'ine villagers and oxide uranium carriers was the result of the probabilistic nature of cancer. The government report received national attention with newspapers concluding that the former workers at the Eldorado Mine had not much to complain about, as the exposure levels to radiation were not high enough to cause cancer.[38] Soon, alternative explanations began surfacing, suggesting that the cancer rates had other causes. Could it be the Dene's notorious smoking habits? The government report upheld a familiar line of argumentation to Indigenous people reaching back to the 1930s. It also led the way for the more recent prospect of reopening the mine, with mining companies strategizing in 2014 on how to deal with First Nation interests.[39] Interestingly, a recent study from 2022 concluded that the "radiation risks of lung cancer among men increased significantly" for workers at the Eldorado mine who were exposed to radiation, thus reverting the scientific conclusion of previous studies.[40]

Rule, and Production of Difference," *Geoforum* 15 (March 2013), 5–16. Brenda Parlee, John O'Neil, and Lutsei K'e Dene First Nation, "'The Dene Way of Life': Perspectives on Health from Canada's North," *Journal of Canadian Studies* 41:3 (2007), 112–133.

37 Canada Deline Uranium Table, *Final Report Concerning Health and Environmental Issues Related to the Port Radium Mine* (Toronto: Government of Canada, 2005), 73, 74, 78.

38 Anonymous, "Uranium Exposure Insufficient to Cause Cancer in Deline Workers: Report," *CBC News: North*, August 12, 2005.

39 Geordan Graetz, "Uranium Mining and First Peoples: The Nuclear Renaissance Confronts Historical Legacies," *Journal of Cleaner Production* 84 (2014), 339–347.

40 Lydia B. Zablotska, Rachel S. D. Lane, and Kristi Randhawa, "Association Between Exposures to Radon and γ-ray Radiation and Histologic Type of Lung Cancer in Eldorado Uranium Mining and Milling Workers from Canada," *Cancer* 128:17 (September 2022), 3135–3266.

The story of the Sahtu Got'ine is not unique. As Winona LaDuke has pointed out, First Nations people hold a significant amount of the world's uranium resources on their land and can as a consequence be linked not only to Hiroshima but "to more than a thousand nuclear tests" in Nevada and the Pacific.[41] In many, if not most, of these cases, optimistic as well as pessimistic prophecies have been rationalized. These are cases of typical settler colonialism, where one part moves in with a vision of prosperity at the expense of an existing lifestyle or culture. As a scholar of Indigenous history, Patrick Wolfe has pointed out, "the process of replacement maintains the refractory imprint of the native counter-claim."[42] The ongoing clash between claims and counter-claims, traditional and scientific knowledge, mark these stories which are rarely resolved. Is it all in the eye of the beholder? Or is it in the power of the best argument? The question remains: why was the environment of the Sahtu Got'ine destroyed in order to create destruction?

As it turns out, the trail of destruction did not end with the Sahtu Got'ene. The bags with uranium were transported to the Eldorado Port Hope refinery where the ore was processed into yellowcake or low-grade uranium powder. Here too, factory workers were exposed to radioactivity, and the environment was damaged. The yellowcake was then sent to the ultra-secret town of Wheat for further enrichment which generated even more havoc. All of which will be the topic of the next chapter.

---

41 Winona LaDuke with Sean Cruz, *The Militarization of Indian Country* (East Lansing: Michigan State University Press, 2012), 37. Bruce E. Johansen, *Resource Exploitation in Native North America: A Plague Upon the Peoples* (Santa Barbara: Praeger, 2016), 1–16.
42 Patrick Wolfe, "Settler Colonialism and the Elimination of the Native," *Journal of Genocide Research* 8:4 (2006), 387–409, 389.

CHAPTER 2

THE WAR ON WHEAT

Once upon a time, there was a small farming community in Roane County, Tennessee, called Wheat. From the earliest settlement in 1789, the people of Wheat lived off land that effectively was stolen from the Shawnee and Yuchi tribes and further developed by slaves. Yet by the late 1930s, this legacy was seen as events of the past by a community whose daily life focused on growing wheat and vegetables, caring for their livestock, berry picking, hunting, and fishing. Their tanning of hides, shoe-making, weaving, knitting, brick-making, and blacksmithing are all evidence of the ways that they created their own homes, clothes, and tools. What cash they needed came from selling produce and cattle. They got clean water from the nearby Poplar Creek, and those living on higher grounds would bring buckets of it to their houses with the help of wires and wheels. At the gristmill, they would grind their grains, and the mailbox on the mill's wall was the community's natural meeting place. Once a year, they would make molasses from sorghum cane so that their children could enjoy some sweet biscuits, after which they would all participate in square dancing. They also took pride in their Wheat School where their children received education. Their lifestyle was not necessarily easy. Indeed, the chief account of the town's history bears evidence of a varied group of people arguing about all those things most people do. Yet Wheat still had a strong sense of community, with people taking care of each other and the land on which they lived.[1]

Every Sunday, the Wheat community would meet at the George Jones Memorial Baptist Church which they had built in 1901 at the McKinney

---

1 Dorathy S. Moneymaker, *We'll call it Wheat* (Oak Ridge: Adroit Printing, 1979). Colbi Layne W. Hogan, *Displaced to Save the World*, Ph.D. thesis (Murfreesboro: Middle Tennessee State University, 2021).

Ridge at the nearby Poplar Creek. The stream was where they would be baptized in a complete immersion of water, a symbolic act of being reborn through the water they all depended on. Judging from the chief historical account of life at Wheat, evangelical Protestantism was at the core of the daily life of most citizens. Their daily prayers may thus capture well the spiritual world in which most of them moved when they would fold their hands and say: "Give us this day our daily bread. And forgive us our debts, as we also have forgiven our debtors. And do not bring us to the time of trial, but rescue us from the evil one."[2]

However, unbeknownst to them, the evil one arrived in the evening of June 30, 1942.

The Destruction of the Wheat Community

The evil one had the best intentions and was driven by the prospect of scientific progress and the possibility of developing nuclear weapons so that the nation could prevail in its wars. The people of Wheat noticed his coming first with the "continuous humming of an airplane circling overhead [...] Day after day [...] creating an eerie feeling of apprehension."[3] Up in the plane was Major General Kenneth D. Nichols. He was sent to the region to survey possible sites for building processing facilities for the enrichment of the uranium, most of which came from the Eldorado Mine in Canada. The aim was to enrich the U-235 (uranium isotope) needed for the bombs. He was looking for a spacious place that had lots of water, access to electricity, proximity to the Southern Railroad, river accessibility, sufficient land to build at least four plants, including homes for their workers, and, most importantly, a place granting both military security and secrecy.[4]

The farmland around the Wheat community provided more or less exactly what he wanted. Its rolling hills could protect the plants from each other in case one exploded or was attacked. The Blackoak Ridge next to the smaller McKinney Ridge and the Pine Ridge provided suitable protection, while the valleys between them, such as the Sugar Grove Valley, Bear Creek Valley, and the East Fork Valley were ideal spots for the factories. There were creeks, shoals, and rivers of water to be used in the plants, and nearby waterways and

---

2 *The Bible*, Matthew 6:9-15. Moneymaker, *We'll call it Wheat*, 1979, 7–8, 45–46, 56.

3 Moneymaker, *We'll call it Wheat*, 1979, iv.

4 Kenneth. D. Nichols, *The Road to Trinity* (New York: William Morrow, 1987), 39.

roads provided relatively easy access. And it was not in a place in which enemy spies would suspect top-secret military research and facilities.

The faith of the Wheat community was sealed at a top-secret meeting of the S-1 Executive Committee on July 30, 1942. This was the committee that laid the groundwork for what soon became the Manhattan Project. The United States, it is worth recalling, had been drawn into the Second World War with the attack on its navy fleet by the Japanese at Pearl Harbor on December 7, 1941. This sent the nation into an intense war effort, which included making everything from the simplest bullet to advanced weaponry. Secret reports from scientists conveyed that Nazi Germany was in the process of developing nuclear weapons, and President Franklin D. Roosevelt made the order that the United States should make every effort to beat them at it. The mission was given the code name the Manhattan Project to focus attention away from where things were happening, and its leaders were given the power to purchase necessary land to build factories and research facilities for the endeavor.

As a result, the Army Corps of Engineers surveyed numerous sites around the nation. For the uranium processing facilities, they landed on the land between Clinch River to the South and Blackoak Ridge to the North in Tennessee as their best option. The 59,000-acre large site included not only Wheat but also parts of the Elza, Robertsville, and Scarborough (now spelled Scarboro) communities. They would be affected in different ways, with Elza and Wheat most severely with the building of factories Y-12 and K-25, respectively, on their land.

In a letter signed on November 11, 1942, the area was taken by the means of eminent domain and residents were told they had to vacate homes and land they had occupied for generations by December 1. Where the order was impossible to deliver, it was simply posted on walls and fences. They "suffered real hardships by their dislocation," the head of the Manhattan Project, General Leslie R. Groves, later admitted.[5] The financial compensation given to the Wheat farmers for their land ($30 an acre) was hardly sufficient to provide similar farmland elsewhere, which inflated in price given the sudden large demand. And the social security of their community and the know-how of how to live with the land they knew were lost. Yet they left their beloved homes with few complaints, seeing it as their patriotic contribution to the war effort. (There was one hold-out who hid in the woods for a year before he too was expelled). "What do you do?" one farmer asked. "The government needed

---

5 Leslie R. Groves, *Now it Can be Told* (New York: Harper, 1962), 26.

your land to win the war. Who would refuse such a request as that?"[6] Indeed altogether 157 men from Wheat joined the military. For a few superstitious farmers, these events did not come as a total surprise. Their local prophet, John Hendrix, had back in 1902 "seen it" coming, predicting that "the earth will shake." "I tell you, Bear Creek Valley someday will be filled with great buildings and factories, and they will help toward winning the greatest war that ever will be."[7]

After the farmers had left, the destruction of Wheat began quickly, and by the fall of 1942, the entire community was erased except for their church which is still there today. The destruction was so complete that not even the name of their community would survive. Instead, historians tend to use the name Oak Ridge anachronistically when describing the area, a name given to the land after the war had ended. It was a name inspired by the ridge next to Wheat, Blackoak Ridge, which indicated the type of oak found in its forest. This key information about the trees was erased when the military named the town, a telling image of how local know-how of how to live with the land was wiped out with the arrival of nuclear research. The eradication of local knowledge was the very precondition for the production of science.

The Destruction of Clinch River

Before the military arrived, the Clinch River meandered through the Wheat community, providing water, fish, and transportation for its farmers. In the spring, the river tended to flood, which could be a yearly cause of headache for the entire region. The river had its origins in faraway Virginia and would, after passing Wheat, eventually lead to the Tennessee River, the Ohio River, and finally to the mighty Mississippi River. For generations, this entire river system had been (and indeed still is) a major route of transportation, occasionally hampered by various river shoals. When the factories were built for the Manhattan Project, the water would supply cooling for its machinery and drinking water for its many workers, and conveniently, it would take away waste and sewage.

The management of the river system was at the heart of the New Deal program initiated by Roosevelt in response to the Great Depression of the 1930s. The most prominent among these programs was the construction of

---

6 Leland Johnson and Daniel Schaffer, "The First 50 Years," *Oak Ridge National Laboratory Review* 25:3/4 (1992), 1–28, quote p. 5.

7 David Ray Smith, *John Hendrix Story* (Knoxville: Lulu, 2013), 5.

the Norris Dam built between 1933 and 1936. It was about a short day's travel from Wheat. Its ability to control the yearly spring flood was the major upside for Wheat farmers. More importantly, the new Norris town made for the dam's construction workers would set the standard for the future of the entire Tennessee Valley, including Wheat. Anyone wondering what the future would entail could just go and visit Norris and also admire the mighty dam.

The chief designer of the Norris Dam was Roland Wank, a young immigrant from Budapest trained as an architect and engineer in the modernist Bauhaus tradition. "Good architecture grows superb under the dramatic effects of the atmosphere and water," he argued, and "what we do to our rivers is part of the energy housekeeping" reflecting "our national spirit and ambition."[8] Wank would give the Norris Dam and its surroundings a distinctly modernist look to reflect a new beginning for a financially depressed region. In this, he followed the overall aim of his employer, The Tennessee Valley Authority (TVA), which was to propel the social and environmental life of the valley into both health and wealth. Their endeavor has been reviewed by the architectural historians Christine Macy and Sarah Bonnemaison, who have shown how everything, from the dam to town planning (including racial segregation), houses, and the natural scenery, was carefully designed to reflect a new harmonious relationship between sublime technology and sublime nature.[9] It was the modernist novelties of Norris that made Wheat look out-of-date to both its citizens and to the Generals who confiscated their land. Thus, the destruction of Wheat became a fulfillment of an imagined historical trajectory that began at Norris, and the speed at which Norris was erected allowed a similar culture of construction and modernization on land confiscated by the Manhattan Project.

From Norris, the Clinch River flowed its natural route in a fairly flat path in the valleys between the ridges, only obstructed by a few river shoals. The shoals were major obstacles for river transportation, and TVA decided to construct the Watts Bar Dam which would create a lake suitable for large boats on

---

8 Roland Wank, "The Architecture of Inland Waterways," in *New Architecture and City Planning*, ed. Paul Zucker (New York: Philosophical Library, 1944), 440–458, quotes on pp. 440, 443. Marian Moffett, "Looking to the Future: The Architecture of Roland Wank," *Arris: Journal of the Southeast Chapters of the Society of Architectural Historians* 1 (1989), 5–17.

9 Christine Macy and Sarah Bonnemaison, *Architecture and Nature: Creating the American Landscape* (New York: Routledge, 2003), 137–221.

the Clinch River up to the Melton shoals (where the Melton Hill Dam is today). The Watts Bar is one of several dams built by TVA in the late 1930s, which would allow the citizens of Wheat uninterrupted water transportation of their cattle and produce. The construction of the Watts Bar began in the summer of 1939 and finished in January 1942, which was one of the reasons why Wheat was an attractive site to the Generals. The new Watts Bar eased the transportation to the Manhattan Project's new factory sites, along with an extension of the railroad to Wheat.

Thus, the modernist onslaughts on the land in the region around Wheat had been going on for almost a decade before the generals arrived in 1942. In the 1930s, TVA initiated a series of land and water reform programs affecting the region, which were made to provide a New Deal for the nation during the Great Depression. The factories the Manhattan Project sought to build at Wheat would, in part, depend on and extend these TVA projects. Building nuclear weapons not only required the destruction of local communities but also of land and waterways in the entire Tennessee Valley, which reaches from southwest Kentucky to north Georgia and from northeast Mississippi to the Virginia and North Carolina mountains. That is, the Manhattan Project had to tap into energy production that already had or was in the process of creating tremendous environmental destruction in the large valley.

They were not the first to think of this region as ideal for warfare production. At Kingsport, north of Norris, the Chemical Warfare Service had barracks and a plant that was producing stockpiles of poison gas just in case it was needed.[10] In the early 1940s, before the veil of secrecy on nuclear weapons production was firmly in place, the press would compare the possible new nuclear weapon to that of poison gas due to its devastatingly wide distribution of "death dust."[11] The use of radioactive "death dust" in warfare was of concern to the Americans who feared that the Germans could produce such bombs. The historian of physics Jimena Canales has pointed out that the possible association between nuclear fallout from atomic bombs with poison gas was something leaders of the Manhattan Project avoided so that the bomb would

---

10 National Archives and Records Administration, folder 165-WW-99A-59, file 26424660. Leo P. Brophy, *The Chemical Warfare Service: From Laboratory to Field* (Washington: Defense Dept. 1982), 334.

11 John W. Campbell, "Is Death Dust America's Secret Weapon?" *PIC Magazine*, July 22, 1941, 6–8.

not be perceived as being in violation of the 1925 Geneva Protocol against chemical warfare.[12] With the modernist construction process, the Clinch River ceased to be a river and became instead Watts Bar Lake (prolonged by Melton Hill Lake after 1963). The floating energy of the river, however, did not disappear but was instead transformed by generators into consumable electricity. This transformation of natural streams into electric power was subject to much fascination, lore, and celebration. The generators making it possible became what anthropologists call "boundary objects" defining a culture. They were worthy of a visit by locals as well as faraway travelers admiring TVA from overseas. The British biologist Julian Huxley may serve as an example. He saw the dams as an example of the successful transformation of the economy of nature in tune with modern planning and functional democracy.[13] He visited Tennessee briefly in 1935, and again in 1941 when he became firmly convinced that the valley could serve as the model for successful reordering and empowerment of the British Empire. What caught Huxley's attention was the comprehensive scale of a plan that saw geography, soil, agriculture, forestry, animal life, recreation, scenery, fishing, technical research, health, commerce, industry, architecture, housing, and design as all part of one grand synchronized project. The virtue of the alteration of the Tennessee Valley was, Huxley argued, the complete reinforcement of the economy of nature (through dams and electrification) which empowered the human ecology. It was, he argued, a project that radically altered the environment and social life in Tennessee, with scientists and lay people living together in social harmony.

The electricity from the Norris Dam and the Watts Bar was important to the building and running of the machinery of the new factories built for the Manhattan Project. The destruction and alteration of the Clinch River ecosystem is what enabled the enrichment of the uranium factories. "Of all the aspects of process support required for the atomic project, none was more vital

---

12 Jimena Canales, "The Secret PR Push That Shaped the Atomic Bomb's Origin Story," *The Atlantic*, April 18, 2017, online.
13 Julian Huxley, *TVA Adventure in Planning* (Surrey: The Architectural Press, 1943); Anonymous, "Work of the Tennessee Valley Authority," *Nature* 152 (July 17 1943), 73. R. Brightman, "Judgment on Planning," *Nature* 153 (April 29 1944), 508–509. William U. Chandler, *The Myth of TVA* (Cambridge: Ballinger Pub., 1984). Walter L. Creese, *TVA's Public Planning* (Knoxville: University of Tennessee Press, 1990).

than electric power," the military historian Vincent Jones rightly notes.[14] It was the currents of the Clinch River that created the electricity, which in turn allowed the enrichment of uranium, which was used to create the chain reaction of the nuclear bombs. Thus, the energy unleashed over Hiroshima could and should be traced back to the slow currents of the Clinch and Tennessee rivers. The destructive power of nuclear bombs was not only blowing up land and cities but also in how they were produced.

The Destruction of the Wheat Land

Turning Wheat's productive farmland into the mud was the first thing the Manhattan Project leadership did after the community had been expelled and their homes had been torn down. The farmland had to be flattened and roads had to be built to prepare for construction. The result was a landscape of sludge which lasted more or less until the end of the war. The construction of buildings, homes, and factories was a chief reason for this, but also the fact that the people moving in did not have the know-how of how to live with the landscape. Greenscaping was foreign to the new settlers, except for the occasional planting of some ornamental shrubs. As a result, people having been in the top secret area during the war would give it away by having mud on their shoes. The mud became a marker—a secret handshake—separating insiders from outsiders of the new secretive site.

Through the mud, new roads emerged, allowing for the transport of building materials and workers from far away. There was a chronic shortage of both with the nation gearing up military production on all fronts and mustering able men as soldiers. Yet the Manhattan Project was given the highest priority with respect to both materials and laborers. After the roads came electric power lines, which connected the site to the TVA grid. This created a security problem. What if a saboteur cut the power line? Or would TVA be able to provide a stable flow of energy in a nation with a chronic shortage of electricity? Even the shortest interruption of electricity could be disastrous for the uranium enrichment factory. As a result, a coal plant empowering a steam turbine using water drawn from the Clinch River was built. It became the largest coal plant in the United States to that date with electric generators providing the factories with a steady flow of electricity. The housing for people working at the factories

14 Vincent C. Jones, *Manhattan: The Army and the Atomic Bomb* (Washington: Center for Military History, 1985), 377.

was also heated by coal. In total, the site used approximately 150,000 kilowatts escalating to 250,000 by the end of the war.

It has been impossible to trace where all the coal came from, but there were several coal mines in the area in the early 1940s which were likely providers, such as ones at the Coal Creek in the north or in the coal-rich Cumberland Mountains to the south. In any case, the large orders of coal for the Manhattan Project must have been a boost to local mining. The excavation of coal would more often than not lead to the destruction of environmental habitat, leaving a trail of everlasting dead markers in the landscape, alongside air pollution. While the physics community often points out the half-life of radioactive isotopes when measuring nuclear contamination, it is telling that the Manhattan Project literature hardly discusses smoke from the burning of coal and the destruction of land caused by mining.

While the workers in the Manhattan Project factories may have been exposed to such pollutants, it is noteworthy that TVA had set up a series of environmental remedies to promote workers' health and well-being. The Great Smoky Mountains National Park was chartered in 1934, along with the construction of the Blue Ridge Parkway, which began in 1935, and the completion of the nearby Appalachian Trail in 1937. Most people working for the Manhattan Project would not enjoy these environments for security reasons, but their very existence nevertheless allowed the destruction of Wheat. The nearby pure, clean, and untouched parks and trails would allow for a culture in which the rest of the landscape could be destroyed.

In the midst of where the people of Wheat had lovingly cultivated their land, the military built a humongous four-story building known as K-25. Indeed, it may have been the largest building built in the United States. The "K" stood for Kellex (a secret military subsidiary of the Kellogg Company that designed it), and "25" was a vague secretive reference to the U-235 uranium isotope. What was needed was highly enriched uranium U-235 that can undergo fission. The best option to generate weapons-grade uranium used in nuclear bombs was deemed to be gaseous diffusion. The process entailed forcing uranium hexafluoride gas through membranes capable of separating molecules containing fission-grade uranium U-235 from uranium U-238. It was a complicated process enriching U-235 gram by gram, with the need for a bomb being in the kilos. (The bomb used to annihilate Hiroshima contained 64 kilos.) The gaseous diffusion process would need a lot of space because the process required many and large cascades of membranes in which each stage would process and purify the uranium until one had high-grade U-235.

FIGURE 2: The K-25 gaseous diffusion plant built on the Wheat community farm-land. The Poplar Creek is in the foreground while the housing units on Wheat's land can be seen in the valley behind the McKinney Ridge forest where the George Jones Memorial Church is also located. Photo: James E. Westcott. Credit: American Museum of Science and Energy/Wikimedia Commons.

For blue-collar workers at the factory, this process was rather mysterious, as they were not told about the tiny amounts of uranium they helped produce. The African Americans at the very bottom of the social ladder thus kept wondering what their work was all about. "They would see huge quantities of material going into the plants but nothing coming out. This created an atmosphere of unreality, in which giant plants operated feverishly day and night to produce nothing that could be seen or touched."[15] The scientists knew what was being produced, of course, while those on the factory floor were mystified.

15 Paul Henderson, "7000 Employed at Atomic Bomb Plant," *Afro-American*, August 18, 1945, 1, 2.

The language of purification associated with this chemical process is deceptive, as there was nothing "pure" about K-25. Instead, the factory and its process of uranium purification left behind a trail of destruction so disastrous that the former Wheat farmland will likely never be farmed again. Indeed, the area was in 1989 designated a national "superfund" environmental disaster site or environmental sacrifice zone with a costly cleanup program scheduled to last until 2047—over 100 years after the production of U-235 began.[16] The destructive power of nuclear bombs was not only in what it did to Hiroshima but also in its everlasting destruction of U.S. soil and groundwater.

The Atom City of Individualism

"When a new place is to be built, the first thing that must be done is to be rid of the old place," a former citizen of Wheat noted tersely when looking back at the historical events.[17] Indeed, thousands of people would move into the erased community of Wheat to build and run the Manhattan Project's factories, accumulating to as many as 75,000 people by the end of the war. About half of them were construction workers, but there were also military and administrative personnel, engineers, cooks, scientists, operation managers, shopkeepers, teachers, cleaners, and so on. With millions of men fighting in the war, the Manhattan Project would actively recruit young women in their workforce.[18] They all had to comply with the military style of social order.

All these people needed places to live, schools for their children, healthcare, shops, and more. The architectural firm Skidmore, Owings and Merrill (SOM) was hired in December 1942 to plan and supervise the construction of the new settlements. Their task was to build for "different individuals transplanted from every part of the country in an unbelievable short time."[19] Due to military secrecy, the architects were initially not given the location of the site. The settlement they began designing was thus for people and a place they

---

16 Charles Openchowski, "The Oak Ridge Cleanup: Protecting the Public or the Polluter?" *Environmental Law Reporter* 53:3 (March 2023), 10188–10211.

17 Moneymaker, *We'll call it Wheat*, 1979, iv.

18 Denise Kiernan, *The Girls of Atomic City: The Untold Story of the Women who Helped win World War II* (New York: Touchstone, 2013).

19 Nathaniel Alexander Owings, *The Spaces in Between* (Boston: Houghton Mifflin, 1973), 84. Louis Falstein, "A Visit to the Secret Town in Tennessee that Gave Birth to the Atomic Bomb," *New Republic* 113 (November 12, 1945), 635–637.

did not know. As a consequence, the architects were forced to submit rather abstract layouts that did not take into account knowledge about the needs of the people and the environment in which they were building. Roads, community buildings, and homes were laid out in a landscape unknown to them with great speed and according to their imagined modernist ideals. This entailed practical difficulties. For example: when SOM put in an urgent order for 15,000 toilet fixtures to be delivered to a small town in Tennessee, the manufacturer thought it must be a misunderstanding. Soon the military realized that the architect John Merrill (the M in SOM) would need security clearance, and he ended up spending considerable time on site, which helped in terms of determining ideal road and house locations. Yet a high level of abstraction in planning the developments would remain when the construction was carried out.

The people of Wheat had left by the time the SOM architects arrived, except for the dead whose graves were off-limits to developments. These graveyards became, in effect, Wheat's revenge of some sort. There were about 10 of them surrounding the K-25 factory, and according to the architects, they tended "to be nestling in the center of a [future] high school gymnasium or between two main road junctions or in some ideally located six-room house." Indeed, SOM felt "defeated" by the cemeteries as they would not allow them to lay out their town according to their high modernist ideals.[20] The dead were inviolate and refused to leave.

The new settlement was located up the valley from the K-25 factory, and it would house about 17,000 people on land formerly known as Wheat. In terms of design, it took on a modernist look similar to the Norris town and other TVA projects, although the SOM architects were not allowed to use much energy on the detailed appearance of the new buildings. Instead, they put all their energy into constructing the town as fast as possible. The project was all about speed with prefabricated homes being put up, literally, on the same day that their plots were marked.

The new homes were given codenames A, B, C, D, and E depending on the social status of its future inhabitants. The layouts of the SOM planning have been scrutinized by the landscape historian Peter Bacon Hales who shows how the most prestigious homes with scenic views were for the scientists and army officers, while remaining where distributed according to class and race

---

20 Owings, *The Spaces in Between*, 1973, 95.

in modest homes, temporary dwelling units, and simple trailers.[21] The homes were placed in scenic or non-scenic locations, or simply by the road, and distributed to their new inhabitants according to their time of arrival, social rank, and racial identity. In the hierarchy of housing, the scientists were on the top of the ladder while unskilled laborers were at the bottom.

The "Negro Village" was located at the lowest swampiest part of the landscape and closest to the factories. The village hosted exactly 10 percent of the workforce, and they consisted of mostly African American workers but also workers of Latin American and Native American descent. They did not live in houses but in simple hutments and had limited or no access to social services. Their segregated recreation facilities were the only place in which fighting and prostitution would be tolerated. This helped to enforce a racist image of non-white workers as brutish and dangerous, and, as a consequence, that it was necessary to separate them from the rest of the population. In this way, racial segregation became a way of creating both black and white identities for a settlement of strangers arriving from different walks of life. As the historian of race, Nell Irvin Painter has shown, the construction of whiteness in the United States was reinforced with modernist post-war housing policies,[22] policies which had their bearings in the Manhattan Project's housing program.

With the annihilation of Hiroshima and the opening up of the secret city to journalists, African American–leaning newspapers reported extensively and with pride on their contribution to the war effort. "7000 Employed at Atomic Bomb Plant" were people of color, the *African American* noted, while also pointing out Jim Crow conditions resulting in very little healthcare and no access to school for their children.[23] The same newspapers would also take pride in the work of African American scientists, including researchers such as Harold Delaney, Harold Evans, Ralph Alexander Gardner, Jasper B. Jeffries, William J. Knox, Edward A. Russell, Benjamin Scott, Moddie Taylor, Jesse E. Wilkins, and many others. These also included female scientists, such as Cynthia Hall, Blanche J. Lawrence, and Carolyn Beatrice Parker, along with

21 Peter Bacon Hales, *Atomic Spaces: Living on the Manhattan Project* (Urbana: University of Illinois Press, 1997), 83–92. George O. Robinson, *The Oak Ridge Story* (Kingsport: Southern Pub., 1950). Charles W. Johnson and Carles O. Jackson, *City Behind a Fence: Oak Ridge, Tennessee 1942-1946* (Knoxville: University of Tennessee Press, 1981).
22 Nell Irvin Painter, *The History of White People* (New York: Norton, 2010), 359–373.
23 Henderson, "7000 Employed at Atomic Bomb Plant," 1945, 1, 2.

other professionals of color.[24] They were recruited mostly from the universities of Chicago and Columbia and worked at different scientific aspects and locations within the Manhattan Project.[25] The same journalists spared no ink letting their readers learn about their achievements as inspirational examples to follow.[26] An editorial even hoped their contributions could help "splitting the atom of race hate" in the United States.[27] Yet the official *Smyth Report* about the Manhattan Project would not mention contributions by scientists of color, focusing instead on all the white scientists, and subsequent historians of the bomb have largely followed suit in silencing them.

The petit-bourgeois ideal of a single-family home would apply to both houses, trailers, and hutments, and a few smaller apartment buildings. Family was the unit of order, and not community or class. With the radical influx of people, the initial town plans with communal structures created by SOM largely disappeared or were corrupted by *ad hoc* solutions and placement of homes. As a result, the chief unity of the town's social order became the family, and not the working class. Although there were churches, schools, boutiques, and recreation facilities, the alphabet homes became the all-important unit of social order. It was designed for families, even though groups of workers without families would live there as much of the workforce was unmarried. Although there is no direct connection to the Manhattan Project, it is telling that it was in this period that sociologists began using the term "nuclear family" in reference to the basic unit or "atom" of society, while in pre-war literature, the term described the society's "cell" or nucleus. In both cases, it

24 Anonymous, "Behind the Men Who Made the Atomic Bomb Were These Women," *Afro-American,* August 18, 1945, 15.

25 Richard Durham, "Negro Scientists Help to Split Atoms," *The Chicago Defender,* August 18, 1945, 1. George Schuyler, "Negro Scientists Played Important Role in Development of Atomic Bomb," *The Pittsburgh Courier,* August 18, 1945, 17. Ted Coleman, "Chicago Men in Spotlight," *The Pittsburgh Courier,* August 18, 1945, 17. National Park Service, *African Americans at Los Alamos and Oak Ridge: A Historic Context Study*, US. Department. of Interior, September 2019.

26 Coleman, "Chicago Men in Spotlight," 1945, 17. Anonymous, "Colored Scientists Aided Atom Study," *Afro-American,* August 18, 1945, 1, 8.

27 Anonymous (editorial), "Splitting the Atom of Race Hate," *The Chicago Defender,* August 18, 1945, 12.

surely describes well the all-important social unit of what eventually became the town of Oak Ridge.[28]

Right after the war, when the first reports about the town were published, it became known as the "Atom City" in a reference to the place's obvious importance for the production of nuclear bombs.[29] The irony is that it was also an atomic city in the sense of the atomic nature of its citizens. The settlement was like a gathering of thousands of self-interested individuals operating as "atoms" without the communal belonging Wheat was originally known for. What social identity they did have was based on racial identity, alphabetical grade of their homes, and nuclear family, in addition to a sense of being involved in the nation's war effort and having pride in the American flag. Built on the ruins of the Wheat community emerged an Atom City of only individuals.

Individualism suits military needs well, as it allows a reordering of people so that they can march according to the General's order. The lack of community also served military planners seeking to protect the U.S. landscape. At the Atomic City, they sought, for security reasons, to separate the factories, the new homes, and other facilities between the ridges in the landscape in case of air attack, sabotage, or accidental explosions or fires. As a result, the individual buildings were not organized as a community centering on the church or grocery store but instead dispersed throughout the landscape with forest areas in between and connected by roads. After the war, the landscape design of Oak Ridge became the norm for how to organize the entire nation in case of nuclear attack. "A good decentralization program would [...] reduce the target attractiveness" in nuclear warfare, a military analyst typically thought.[30] Effective nuclear defense of the nation required dispersion of the population to the countryside where individuals or nuclear families ideally should live in

---

28 George Peter Murdock, "Anthropology and Human Relations," *Sociometry* 4 (1941), 140–149. Daniel Scott Smith, "The Curious History of Theorizing about the History of the Western Nuclear Family," *Social Science History* 17:3 (1993), 325–353.

29 Daniel Lang, "Atom City," *Architectural Forum* 83:4 (October 1945), 103–116; "The Atomic City," *The New Yorker*, September 29, 1945, 48–55. S. Adkins, "Birthplace of the Atomic Bomb," *Architectural Record* 98 (September 1945), 10–13.

30 Ralph E. Lapp, *Must we Hide?* (Cambridge: Addison-Wesley Press, 1949), 165. Sylvan G. Kindall, *Total Atomic Defense* (New York: Richard R. Smith Pub., 1952), 84–85. Peter Galison, "War against the Center," in *Architecture and the Sciences*, ed. Antoine Picon and Alessandra Ponte (New York: Princeton Architectural Press, 2003), 196–227. Elaine Tyler May, *Fortress America: How We Embraced Fear and Abandoned Democracy* (New York: Basic Books, 2017), 13–56.

dispersed homes while also nurturing the ability to survive in the wilderness. Large dense cities, on the other hand, could be attractive targets for the enemy or also nurture a sense of class associated with socialism. Modernist architects followed suit by training their students in such town and landscape planning. At the Institute of Design in Chicago, for example, the architect Richard Buckminster Fuller taught students how to design "decentralized communities" in the event of nuclear warfare.[31]

Throughout the 1950s and beyond, the Atomic City of Oak Ridge became the nation's ideal for town planning, landscape, and suburban design, along with the city of Richland at the Hanford site for plutonium manufacturing where similar ideals emerged.[32] Security in the atomic age, as Elaine Tyler May and others have shown, was intrinsically linked with the family unit living in houses dispersed in the landscape. To live in a closed-knit village, large apartment complexes, or even a city, entailed being a nuclear target, and the government on both national and local levels planned accordingly.[33]

To the scientists, the landscape designs at Oak Ridge were a successful example of how highly specialist chemists and technicians could blossom in a clean environment outside of dirty cities. With the end of the war, there was talk about closing the Atomic City, and the prospect of such a peaceful place being abandoned filled town and country planners with dismay. Instead, the place could perhaps serve as an inspiration for building a new environmentally friendly relationship between scientists and laypeople living in harmony with the surrounding landscapes, town planners imagined.[34]

In sum, the enrichment of U-235 at the Atomic City of Oak Ridge not only destroyed the Wheat community but also water systems and farmland creating everlasting environmental havoc. Even more significantly, it reinforced a social order of individualism with the dispersion of homes for the nuclear family at the cost of a closer woven social fabric. The war on Hiroshima was the result of

---

31 Richard Buckminster Fuller, "New Directions," *Perspecta* (Summer 1952), 29–37, quotes p. 33.

32 Kate Brown, *Plutopia: Nuclear Families, Atomic Cities, and The Great Soviet and American Plutonium Disasters* (Oxford: Oxford University Press, 2013).

33 May, *Fortress America*, 13–44. Thomas Bishop, *Every Home a Fortress: Cold War Fatherhood and the Family Fallout Shelter* (Boston: University of Massachusetts Press, 2020). Laura McEnaney, *Civil Defense Begins at Home: Militarization Meets Everyday Life in the Fifties* (Princeton: Princeton University Press, 2000).

34 Anonymous, "Oak Ridge - A New Town Planned for Destruction," *Town and Country Planning* 13 (1945-1946), 183–185.

the multifaceted war on the Wheat community. The moral fabric of working-class solidarity and communal living with the land was replaced with a culture of individualism brought together by racial identities, military or scientific status, along with pride in the nation's flag and martial mission.

For all the havoc that was wrought, it is notable that the people of Wheat did not fully break up as a community. Their social and environmental bond to the land was too deep. They regularly visited their loved ones in the graveyards after security restrictions were lifted, a custom that has continued to this day, as there are recent graves and fresh flowers in their cemeteries. Indeed, an old farmer—known as the Ghost of Wheat—has refused to leave as he keeps haunting the radioactive wasteland.[35] On every first Sunday in October since 1945, the people of Wheat would hold a reunion in their bellowed George Jones Memorial Baptist Church, the only building standing from their once thriving community. They would meet yearly with their last recorded reunion being in 2014.[36] Here they would turn to the text that meant the most to them, fold their hands, and end their prayer asking the Lord to help them forgive all the trespassing: "For if you forgive others their trespasses, your heavenly Father will also forgive you; but if you do not forgive others, neither will your Father forgive your trespasses."[37]

Yet the unforgiving trespassing would continue, as the now enriched uranium got transported to new research facilities and locations until it was finally assembled into a bomb. That destructive history has been told many times, so it's not worth repeating it here. The result of it all was the annihilation of two cities in Japan, causing endless suffering that is still ongoing. While the Japanese would suffer the brunt of nuclear weapons, it is worth noting that those living downwind from the nuclear disaster sites in the United States were also impacted and would suffer from cancers and related diseases. What is less discussed, is the damaging impact the nuclear bomb made on U.S. culture, including the male gaze on women, which will be the topic of the next chapter.

---

35 Lindsey A Freeman, "Atomic Childhood Around 1980," *Memory Studies* 9 (2016), 75–84, p. 81.
36 Anonymous, "Wheat Community Celebrates Annual Homecoming Sunday," *The Oak Rider*, October 2, 2014.
37 *The Bible*, Matthew 6:9-15.

CHAPTER 3

THE SEX BOMB

Two days after the destruction of Hiroshima, beautiful burlesque "Atomic Bomb Dancers" entertained a thrilled Los Angeles audience at the Burbank variety theater.[1] While people were still dying from radioactive blisters in the ruins of the city, Hollywood had turned the event into good publicity. The death of about 200,000 people was only one month away when *Life* magazine unleashed the "Anatomic Bomb" Starlet Linda Christians on its readers. Lying gracefully on the curving edge of a swimming pool in an "unexplosive moment," she was portrayed as bringing "the new atomic age to Hollywood."[2] She was the all-powerful weapon film producers planned to let loose in the movie theaters. And with no small success, Christians had a thriving career known as the "Anatomic Bomb Girl" well into the 1950s.[3]

Such gendering of nuclear weapons was not new. It began with the bomb named "Little Boy" that was used to annihilate Hiroshima. The plane that dropped it, Enola Gay, was baptized by its captain Paul Tibbets in honor of his mother Enola Gay Tibbets, thus creating an image of his mother "birthing" a new brother of him, a Little Boy, over the Japanese city. That image would change by the end of the war with the bomb itself (as opposed to the plane) being female. In these images of the bomb, the female is destructive in her immense attraction (as in being a "sex bomb"), whereas the male is the victim of her overpowering beauty. Less common, but still familiar, are expressions of having a "fallout" from the "nuclear family," "radiant" personalities, "explosive sex," or someone's reputation being "contaminated." While some of these

---

1 Anonymous, "Right up to Date," *Piqua Daily Call*, August 8 1945, 1.
2 Anonymous, "Anatomic Bomb," *Life* 19:10 (September 3, 1945), 53–54. Starlet Linda Christians' real name was Blanca Rose Welter.
3 Anonymous, "Atomic Anatomy," *Pacific Stars and Stripes*, August 2, 1950, 2.

words were in use before August 1945, nuclear weaponry would boost such vocabulary into everyday usage.

How is it that being compared to something as destructive as nuclear bombs ever became an analogy for romance, compliments, and sexual fantasies? Newspaper cuttings and commentaries in popular magazines show that female bodies in the first decade after the war were portrayed in the language of nuclear weaponry. Their sexiness helped to tame and doll up the portrayal of gruesome bombs in the public imagination. In the process, horrific nuclear weapons became attractive with a ring of illicit adventure, a fetishized object of male empowerment.

Miss Atom Bomb

By the fall of 1945, the war was over, and Japan was trying to heal itself politically, socially, and physically through a productive relationship with its former enemy. Hiroshima and Nagasaki were in ruins and the cities' survivors were left emotionally wrecked with disfigured bodies and horrifying radioactive scars. With their physical health and beauty gone, the young could hardly hope to get married or start a family any time soon. The struggle of daily life was harsh with there being a constant shortage of basic goods like food and clothing.

It was in this context the United States occupying forces in Nagasaki came up with the idea of arranging a Miss Nagasaki Beauty Contest to attempt to cheer up the city and entertain themselves. The event, reviewed by the historian Masako Nakamura, took place in May 1946 and was held in a military hall in front of a panel of all-male judges. The military audience of over a thousand males enjoyed a spectacle of 80 beautiful women competing. The contest was set in a culture in which both Japanese and U.S. authorities made "comfort women" available for soldiers.[4] (When off-duty, some of them would get wasted on cheap wine or a methylated drink called "atom bombo" which may be the first use of slang for getting "bombed" by alcohol.[5]) Yet unlike erotic entertainers and prostitutes, the contestants were fashioned as respectable females dressed in traditional clothing ready to marry and rebuild the

---

4 John Lie, "The State as Pimp: Prostitution and the Patriarchal State in Japan in the 1940s," *The Sociological Quarterly* 38:2 (1997), 251–263.

5 Anonymous, "Metho-Lemon Atom Bombo Blamed For Theft," *Truth*, April 28, 1946, 21.

city. The event was widely reported in the local press, with journalists describing the women in a language of celebration and pride, but without mentioning anything nuclear.

The English-speaking servicemen would typically read the newspaper *Pacific Stars and Stripes* as their chief source of information. They also covered the beauty contest describing the event as a show of friendship between nations: "For once the Marines and the Japanese are in accord. Three Leathernecks of the 10th Marine Regiment joined with six Japanese judges and one Frenchman to cast a unanimous vote for a young Japanese schoolgirl as 'Miss Atom Bomb'."[6] The article created the impression that all parties, including the Japanese, embraced the occupation but also the use of nuclear weapons with a lighthearted labeling of a beautiful woman after it. The expensive clothing of the winner, the 19-year-old Yamamura Yoko, also created the misleading impression that women in Nagasaki had access to such luxuries. Indeed, it is unlikely Yoko was in the city when the bomb was dropped, as she was a graduate of a Japanese school in China. In any case, the beauty contest and the military reporting of it came to fashion the city in the image of their wishful thinking: Nagasaki was thriving, collaboration was working, U.S. occupation was unproblematic, and, most importantly, there was no trauma associated with the use of a nuclear weapon. After all, the people of Nagasaki had fêted the weapon by crowning their own stunning Miss Atom Bomb.

Gilda the Bomb

The U.S. military was also occupying the Pacific islands of the former Japanese Empire, and in the spring of 1946, they began preparing for the first post-war nuclear explosion to take place at the Bikini Atoll. The military personnel at the Kwajalein Atoll Army Garrison would follow their colleagues in Nagasaki, and crown their own "Atomic Queen" among their wives and girlfriends to celebrate the destruction of Bikini.[7] The bombing involved military colonization of foreign territory, forced removal of Indigenous people, and the ecological

---

6 Quoted in Masako Nakamura, "'Miss Atom Bomb' Contests in Nagasaki and Nevada: The Politics of Beauty, Memory, and the Cold War," *U.S.-Japan Women's Journal* 37 (2009), 117–143. Philip R. Wax, "Nagasaki School Girl Crowned 'Miss Atom Bomb,'" *Pacific Stars and Stripes*, May 16, 1946.
7 Lauren Hirshberg, *Suburban Empire: Cold War Militarization in the Pacific* (Berkley: California University Press, 2022), 56.

annihilation of the Atoll, events that will be the topic of the next chapter. It was all reported by a keen press corps which provided regular upbeat accounts based on whatever information the military provided them with.

A popular movie that spring was *Gilda* starring Rita Hayworth as the femme fatale. "Put the blame on Mame," she sang flirtatiously at the end of the film wearing a most beautiful low-necked black evening gown. The scene made the nuclear research personnel stationed at Kwajalein particularly excited. After having seen *Gilda*, the scientists and officers glued an image of Hayworth in that black evening gown on the nuclear bomb designated for Bikini. And then they christened the bomb *Gilda*.[8] Her acting "kept us awake at night," a scientist explained, while the co-pilot designated to drop the bomb jokingly added: "Let's wait and see the detonation."[9]

Hayworth was delighted by having her image on the bomb, as she took great pride in both the scientists and the military personnel involved in the nuclear program. "Since learning that I'm sort of mascot for the Bikini flyers I've been walking on air," she told journalists.[10] There were ulterior motives for her joy, as all the press from her being a mascot put *Gilda* back into the theaters where it made an additional million dollars in gross income.[11] Yet to understand her delight only as financial would be to miss the point. For Hayworth, it was a compliment to her as an actress to have her image on the bomb that decimated the Bikini Atoll. It reinforced the explosive nature of the role she played as a hazardous femme fatale.

The Bikini Swimsuit

In Paris, the fashion designer Luis Reard read about the nuclear explosion at the Bikini Atoll on July 1st and was inspired. He had been working on a new daring swimsuit reflecting the sense of joy and freedom Parisians felt with the end of the war. He launched his new swimsuit under the name "bikini" on July 5, 1946. It was branded as "the smallest bathing suit in the world" made

---

8 Anonymous, "Test Bomb Named 'Gilda'," *New York Times,* June 30 1946, 3. Naming scientist was Thomas Lanahan from the Manhattan Project.
9 Anonymous, "Bomb Called 'Gilda'," *Launceston Examiner,* July 1 1946, 1.
10 Rita Hayworth quoted in Anonymous, "The 'Gilda' Bomb," *Berkeley Daily Gazette,* June 29, 1946, 1.
11 Wood Soanes, "Agent Says Born Yesterday's Producer's Best Success," *Oakland Tribune,* July 23, 1946, 6.

from just thirty inches of fabric.[12] No respectable fashion model in Paris would wear such a thing, so Reard hired instead a striptease dancer from Casino de Paris named Micheline Bernardini to wear it for the annual Most Beautiful Swimmer competition. A tiny swimsuit worn by that kind of a model was slated to cause a stir, which propelled the bikini into fame in Parisian fashion circles. In the first couple of years, the outfit was considered scandalous, and thus rarely mentioned in fashion magazines. It was a high-couture item for underground chic, embodying a libertine culture that sprung loose after years of wartime oppression. The bikinis were controversial and banned from some public swimming pools, as in the case of London where such "blown-to-a-shred" bathing suits were deemed improper. Some women took offense, while others saw them as liberating. For example, in 1950, an angry group of twenty "near-nude bathing bellies" threatened to march on Westminster to get the bikini ban lifted.[13]

What made the swimsuits novel and daring was that they exposed the belly button: "They call them bikinis for they don't cover them atoll," a journalist explained.[14] It's worth reflecting shortly on what's going on here. The outfit exposes the epicenter of the famous Vitruvian model of humans, the midpoint of the age-old artistic expression of the body. At the same time, the analogy between a woman's navel and the atoll in the sea evokes the ancient idea of the Earth being female, with the stomach representing the Pacific Ocean. Indeed, such imagery of "mother earth" harkens back to Greek and Roman ideas of Aphrodite or Venus (the goddess of love and beauty), with the attractive woman in a bikini being the latest incarnation of a long European history of analogies between the female body and the Earth. Both the woman and the Earth are objects of male desire, conquer, love, or also destruction.

No wonder then that the bikini would be described in flattering words. "They're Atomic," a journalist typically noted when bikinis were introduced in a fashion shoot on Miami Beach in the spring of 1948.[15] They are "proving that Bikini is more than a test spot for the atom bomb" noted another journalist

---

12 Patric Alac, *The Bikini: A Cultural History*, trans. Mike Darton (New York: Parkstone Press, 2002), 20–21. Teresia K. Teaiwa, "Bikinis and other s/pacific n/oceans," *Contemporary Pacific* 6 (1994), 87–109.

13 Anonymous, "Westminster Worried: 'Bikini' Belles Baffle Borough," *Winnipeg Free Press*, June 20, 1950, 10.

14 Quoted in Kelly Killoren Bensimon, *The Bikini Book* (New York: Assouline Publishing, 2006), 18.

15 Anonymous, "They're Atomic," *Long Beach Press*, May 8, 1948, 2.

from the same event.[16] Such analogies between the model in the swimsuit and the Bikini Atoll being "tested" by nuclear weaponry continued in the following years, at times with articles about actual nuclear bombing in the Pacific and modeling of bikini swimwear appearing in the same issue of a newspaper. Military news about the power of destruction and fashion news about the power of beauty lived side by side and reinforced each other by using the same language. When the bikinis were introduced on the runway in New York in October 1949 as part of the fashion industry's preparation for the 1950 summer swimsuit collections a reporter could not hold back the enthusiasm. "Like the A-bomb exploded off the island for which the outfit is named, the daring swimsuit created quite a sensation."[17] Indeed, the new swimsuit seemed too daring for the mass market and concerns were also raised about its wearability. Could it fall off? To prove that they were safe, pictures were circulated by designers of a gymnastic ballerina doing back flips on Miami Beach in her bikini.[18] It did not solve the issue, as French women apparently had hips better suited for them.[19] Indeed, a long debate follows the history of bikinis on whether they require a special physique or encourage anorexia, bulimia, and other eating disorders.[20] The real concern in the early 1940s, although, was of the moral kind, with leading fashionista arguing "that the American girl prefers to abandon the 'naked look.'"[21] "French girls can wear them if they want to," Miss America 1949 noted with distaste.[22]

It was exactly the daring nature of the bikinis that made them iconic outfits for every generation since they were first introduced. Indeed, today they are so popular that the name "bikini" will bring up bathing suits before the Pacific Atoll on search engines. This flood of online bikini-dressed female models masks and erases the troubled history of the atoll, giving the destruction of Bikini a ring of exciting attractive beach life.

16 Anonymous, "Proving that Bikini is more than a Test Spot," *Berkeley Daily Gazette*, June 16, 1948, 21.

17 Anonymous, "New 'Bikini' Suit," *Naugatuck Daily News*, October 27, 1949, 5.

18 Anonymous, "Wanting to Prove it's Safe to Move Around in a Bikini," *Washington Evening Journal*, November 27, 1949, 8. Anonymous, "It's Safe to Move," *Austin Sunday American Statesman*, November 26, 1949, 46; *Van Wert Times Bulletin*, November 24, 1949, 9.

19 Anonymous, "She's Outgrown it!" *Dixon Evening Telegraph*, February 16, 1950, 12. Anonymous, "The Trouble with the Bikini," *Life*, September 12, 1949, 65–66.

20 Thomas G. Cole, "(The) Bikini: EmBodying the Bomb," *Genders* 53 (2011), 1–38.

21 Anonymous, "Nude Look on Way Out," *Long Beach Independent*, December 17, 1949, 38.

22 Anonymous, "Miss America Stops in Paris," *Los Angeles Times*, August 7, 1949, 1.

The Nuclear Glitz

In early January 1951, the U.S. military began the nuclear bombardments in Nevada that lasted until 1992, which created large ecological disaster sites and sacrifice zones, including lasting radioactive impact and damage to the soil, water, and ecosystems in the area. The Nevada Proving Grounds is a 680-square-mile area in a desert environment about an hour's drive northwest of Las Vegas, which President Harry Truman established in 1950 to advance nuclear weaponry. First came five bombs under the name "Operation Ranger" (1951), then another series of seven "Operation Buster Jungle" bombs (1951), and then another eight "Operation Tumbler Snapper" bombs (1952), and so on. Indeed, the Nevada Proving Grounds came to endure altogether at least 1021 explosions of which 921 were underground. The aboveground nuclear blasts took place before the Partial Test Ban Treaty of 1963 took effect, and became public spectacles.

The mushroom clouds from the bombs could be seen for a hundred miles or so, making them visible from the windows of downtown hotels in Las Vegas. And their trembling served as noticeable seismic special effects for the thrills of casino tourism. Many of the bombs were intentionally set off at dawn so that the blasts would light up like a sunset, creating a glowing backdrop for a glitzy audience. At the rooftop, the hotels would create nuclear parties where guests could enjoy a drink while looking at the nuclear blast, before continuing to the casinos downstairs. The combination of bomb tourism and gambling made Las Vegas into a boomtown (pun intended) with mobsters and military personnel mingling comfortably, both benefitting from the same blasts.

Many tourists would opt for watching the explosions up close, and the hotels arranged trips to the Mercury village and its nearby observation ridge overlooking the Yucca Flats where the bomb would silently await. Behind thick sunglasses, and at a safe distance, the tourists would have a thrill. A loudspeaker would begin the countdown at thirty minutes and end with the final seconds 10 ... 9 ... 8 ... 7 ... 6 ... 5 ... 4 ... 3 ... 2 ... 1. Boom! "[T]he whole thing is quite a show," the famous ecologist Eugene Odum wrote in his enthusiastic account of seeing the "atomic sunrise."[23] He was one of the numerous visitors, and a telling example of the uncritical gaze even the best scientists had

---

23 Eugene Odum, October 8, 1957, letter to colleagues at University of Georgia. Quoted in Betty Jean Craige, *Eugene Odum: Ecosystem Ecologist and Environmentalist* (Athens: University of Georgia Press, 2001), 69–70.

when observing the ecological destruction of a habitat that, as a result, became one of the most contaminated radioactive environments in the world.

Atomic Vegas Beauties

Atomic beauty pageants and bomb tourism were popular activities in the context of military research by means of nuclear blasts. There were at least four of these pageants, and they were all informal arrangements reflecting the joyful nature of Las Vegas nuclear watch parties and showgirls. They made nuclear detonations innocent and attractive for tourists.

The first winner of such a pageant was Candyce King, or "Candy Kain" as she was known among U.S. military personnel.[24] She was a dancer and showgirl from the Last Frontier Hotel where she would sell high-end diamonds hanging on her bikini at the poolside.[25] In 1952, the hotel arranged one of their atomic blast picnics, and she was slated to entertain. Among the guests were convention participants from the New Mexico Hairdressers and Cosmetologists Association who made a special hair-do for her: "Her hair was brushed into a mushroom explosion shape and had 'steam' rising from it. The steam was vapor produced by dry ice."[26] In this merry outfit, she saw the bomb explode, after which she greeted the military personnel involved. "Radiating loveliness instead of deadly atomic particles, Candyce King [...] dazzled U.S. Marines who participated in recent atomic maneuvers at Yucca Flats. They bestowed on her the title of 'Miss Atomic Blast,' finding her as awe-inspiring in another way, as was the 'Big Bomb.'"[27] The Marines were not the only ones admiring King. Among the tourists peeping at her beauty was a delegation from the Pennsylvania Mushroom Growers Association. Thrilled by her entertainment and the mushroom cloud from the blasts, they bestowed on her a bag of ten pounds of mushrooms.

"The Atomic City" was the theme for the beauty pageant and parade arranged by the North Las Vegas Chamber of Commerce the following year, in 1953. And Paula Harris won the pageant and sat smiling at the top of the chamber of commerce's float beneath a large mushroom cloud. As the nuclear beauty queen of the year, she was crowned "Miss A-Bomb."

---

24 Anonymous, "Hail to the Queen!" *Nevada State Journal,* January 9, 1954, 23.

25 Anonymous, "2.000.000 Worth," *Madison Wisconsin State Journal,* October 11, 1952, 23.

26 Anonymous, "Yucca Shaped Hair-Do," *Albuquerque Tribune,* May 5, 1952, 9.

27 Anonymous, "Miss Atomic Blast," *Walla Union Bulletin,* May 8, 1952, 14.

By 1955, there seems to have been some sort of tradition in place for naming showgirls after nuclear explosions. This time around, military servicemen gave Linda Lawson a tiara made of wire and cotton bunting shaped like a mushroom cloud. Wearing the fashionable "bullet bra" she worked at the Copacabana Room which was an entertainment nightclub at Sands Hotel in Las Vegas. The "Copa Girls" were famous for their beauty, and their club had a series of notable performers such as Frank Sinatra, Count Basie, Ella Fitzgerald, and many more. The Sands Hotel distributed photos to the press of "Miss Cue," a play on the "Operation Cue" aboveground nuclear bombardment. This military research aimed at learning more about the effect of nuclear warfare on everyday life, such as houses, food, clothes, and much more. In the bomb's proximity, there were thus model homes and cars and fashionably dressed plastic mannequins ready for destruction. High winds delayed Operation Cue, and Miss Cue (as in "miscue") was a result of the hotel having to find entertainment for impatient nuclear tourists. She was a "Miss Take," joked a columnist later, thinking she was not really up to par.[28] Nevertheless, her nuclear baptism became the beginning of Lawson's career, as she, in the following years, became a well-known actress.

Finally, there was the case of Lee A. Merlin, another Copa Girl. She entertained in lieu of the "Operation Plumbbob," which was a series of nuclear blasts conducted between May 28 and October 7, 1957. She modeled for the Las Vegas News Bureau's photographer who took an image of her with a cotton mushroom cloud attached to her swimsuit. Known as "Miss Atomic Bomb," the image was widely published and is today perhaps the most famous one in the genre. Journalists described her as their "choice survivor" and "the girl they would most like to survive the A-bomb."[29] The photo visualized what had been tacit all along, namely the location of the bomb's explosion within a woman's vulva resulting in the radiant rise within her body of an imaginary mushroom cloud that culminated around her breasts with the result being a burst of joyful laughter.

Las Vegas was not the only place celebrating Miss Atomic Bombs, nor was the title used only for women of a certain age. Although it's impossible to track all appearances, it's illustrating that as early as 1948 the Hollywood actress Mabel Hart, age 66, labeled herself as "Miss Atomic Bomb of 1890!" due to

---

28 Art Ryon, "Ham on Ryon," *Los Angeles Times,* July 12, 1957, B5.
29 Anonymous, "Choice Survivor," *New Castle News,* June 3, 1957, 5. Similarly in Keokuk Daily Gate City, June 11, 1957, 36, and in *Leesburg Lee County Journal*, May 30, 1957, 1.

FIGURE 3: Miss Atomic Bomb, Lee A. Merlin, 1957. Photo: Don English. Credit: LVCVA Archive.

her good looks.[30] And in 1953, there was a children's beauty pageant in which Patsy Nylander, age four, won the title "Miss Atom Bomb" in Greenfield, Massachusetts. Of all the Bombs, Nylander was the only one who seemed "bored with the whole affair."[31]

The Sex Bomb

From 1950, the press made explicit associations between "sex" and "bomb," thus upping the ante in lexical dramaturgy. To describe a woman as a "bombshell" had already entered the common language since the end of the war, while also being in use before that. An article in *Esquire* about a "Bombshell from Brooklyn" from 1947, for example, describes a model of particular beauty.[32]

---

30 Frank Niell, "Around Hollywood," *New Castle News*, April 15, 1948, 18.

31 Anonymous, "Yipee! I Won," *Ironwood Daily Globe*, October 8, 1953, 8.

32 Jack Moffitt, "Bombshell from Brooklyn: Olga San Juan," *Esquire* 28:2 (January 8, 1947), 37.

What bombshells and sex bombs had in common were being young, white females and more often than not, blond. There were exemptions, of course, although the general trend seems clear: the whiter and blonder the models, the closer association with atomic sexiness. It is as if the image of the white cloud from the nuclear detonation was transformed into a woman's white skin color and blond hair.

Atomic sexiness was also very much the imagination of the film industry, as almost all mentioning of "bombshells" and "sex bombs" are in articles related to movies. These expressions thus belonged in the realm of erotic fantasies and not as the language used in describing, say, good-looking workers, students, politicians, or housewives. Nuclear detonations happened elsewhere at a closed military site in Nevada or in the faraway Pacific, similar to the sex bombs that typically appeared for lay people in print or on a screen.

Sex bombs were also portrayed as dim. Although building nuclear bombs required the best brains of the nation, the bomb itself would strike its victims and environments with an enormous obtuse blast. Similarly, the sex bombs, when effective, would seduce mass audiences by unambiguous anatomical means. To be judged only by your physique could be upsetting to actresses and models who thought they also had intelligence to offer. The actress Betty Hutten, for example, took pride in her being known in the early 1950s as the "blond bombshell," although she was offended about people thinking she had little education. Being well-versed in the classics, she hired her press agent to spread the word that she could read books.[33] Her voice of resistance was an exception.

The film critic Hedda Hopper was probably the one who coined the "sex bomb" phrase. She was a moderately successful actress and politically conservative, who, with 35 million readers of her weekly columns, was an author to reckon with in Hollywood. In 1950, she began promoting Marilyn Monroe, who at the time was only known for minor film roles. The producers should "take a look at our new sex bomb," she advised.[34] Monroe did indeed get their attention, and the result was her breakthrough appearance in *As Young as You Feel* (1951) where she plays a seductive curvaceous private secretary. "Ten to one, you know Hollywood's Marilyn Monroe as Miss Atomic Bomb," the press

---

33 Anonymous, "This Side of Happiness," *Time* 55:17 (April 24, 1950), 68.
34 Hedda Hopper, "Niven Plays the Stars," *Rocky Mount Evening Telegram*, November 2, 1950, 9. Similarly in *Altoona Mirror*, November 2, 1950, 28.

would write about her.[35] By 1951, Hopper was promoting a competing actress, Camille Picket, "to the big guns [of Hollywood]. She's a sex bomb if I ever saw one."[36] Although both Monroe and Picket pitched their acting to a male audience, it is notable that they were promoted as sex bombs by a female author. Initially, the phrase was a female's label of another.

Yet it was Monroe that became most closely associated with the phrase. She became such a powerful bomb that by the mid-1950s other less known bombs would try to distinguish themselves as different from her. There was the "fiery [...] Yugoslav Sex Bomb,"[37] the Greek "sex-bomb"[38] and an invite to see "Europe's biggest sex bomb in all-out explosion. The devastation is impressive."[39] As a result of the growing distribution of television sets, viewers could also enjoy the first "TV sex-bomb."[40] The inflation of the phrase led to an arms race of superlatives. Soon every aspiring actress would claim the title, or be its "prototype."[41] And then the bomb would finally detonate, resulting in "pure, explosive sex."[42] All this would cause some head-shaking among more experienced players. "Please understand that I am all through with this blonde-bombshell business," the movie star Shelly Winters told interviewers in 1956. With her image diluted by cheap ready-to-launch bombs, "veteran lovers of the blonde-bombshell image [...] folded their notes in solemn shame."[43]

The inflation of sex bombs allowed the rise of what may be the first (and only?) male bombshell of the period, the actor William Holden. Starring in the film *Picnic* (1955), he was "a sex bomb" knocking out his female audience. The

35 Anonymous, "Marilyn is Two Girls," *Long Beach Press Telegram,* June 9, 1951, 82–83.

36 Hedda Hopper, "Looking at Hollywood," *Rocky Mount Evening Telegram,* July 35, 1951, 31. Similarly in *Altoona Mirror,* July 25, 1951, 4, in *Salt Lake Tribune,* July 24, 1951, 12, and in *San Antonio Express,* July 24, 1951, 8.

37 Jack Hess, "Fiery Yugoslavian Actress," *Lubbock Morning Avalanche,* May 1, 1954, 62. Model: Elma Carlova.

38 Clyde Gilmore, "Maclan's Movies," *Maclean's Magazine,* May 10, 1958, 38. Model: Melina Mercouri

39 Anonymous, "The New Pictures," *Time* 64:14 (October 4, 1954), 100. Model: Gina Lollobrigida.

40 Anonymous, "'Cool' Welcomes a TV Sex-bomb," *Cool for Cats,* February 28, 1959, 15. Actress Barbara Ferris.

41 John Withcomb, "Miss Exquisite Legs," *Cosmopolitan,* June 1957, 70–71. Prototype: Janis Paige.

42 Anonymous, "Hollywood Today," *Austin Daily Herald,* April 18, 1957, 12. Jean Simmons "explodes" with Paul Newman in *Until They Sail,* 1957.

43 Robert W. Marks, "In Search of Shelly Winters," *Esquire* 46:2 (August 1, 1956), 54–57.

drama describes what happens "after he explodes on a small Midwestern town one summer day. Every woman in the vicinity [...] falls flat, or wants to."[44] This reversal of gender narrative was atypical, and it confirms the general trend of bombshells being women.

The first African American actress described as a bomb was Dorothy Dandridge. The occasion was her controversial lead role in *Island in the Sun* (1957) where she romantically embraces a white gentleman. The script had to be revised many times to pass the censorship of the Motion Picture Production Code, as interracial relationships were proscribed. When a reviewer of the film suggested that she was a bombshell, it was, in effect, a stand in favor of the civil rights movement. The full title of an article about her illustrates this, as the author crossed out: "~~Sexy sultry seductive~~ No she's the SERIOUS BOMBSHELL."[45] Unlike cheap suspicious bombs, Dandridge was morally admirable, suggesting the possibility that the power of her beauty could blow up racial prejudices.

Finally, there was Brigitte Bardot. In France, there was no film censorship. As a consequence, she could do things on the screen that no American actress would even attempt. And she did it in *And God Created Women* (1956). There she acted out explicit nude sexual scenes, all of which were edited away for the American audiences. The infamous dance scene, however, was there for all to see. To the sound of Caribbean rhythms, she erupts into an erotic rapture while dancing with Saint Tropez musicians of color, thus breaking an interracial taboo. At that moment her scorned husband (with whom she had been unfaithful) draws his gun. Bardot became an overnight sensation who propelled the film to fourth place in the American box office in 1957. "Her sex-bomb reputation" would from now on challenge that of Monroe.[46] Mutually they came to reinforce an image of bombshells being blond, curvaceous young women.

Radiating Nuclear Families

The sex bombs were objects of both desire and fear. In the role of femme fatale, they owned the power to possess, conquer, and destroy a man's will, family

---

44 Anonymous, "The Conquest of Smiling Jim," *Time* 67:19 (February 27, 1956), 63.
45 Anonymous, "~~Sexy sultry seductive~~. No she's the SERIOUS BOMBSHELL," *Picturegoer*, Jul. 20. 1957, 14–15. Leslie Uggams is a later example of an African-American bombshell, as in Anonymous, "Leslie, a Cool Bombshell," *Life*, June 23, 1967, 84–90.
46 Peter Basch, "The Child Women of Europe," *Cosmopolitan* 144 (June 1958), 46–53, quote on p. 47.

values, and sense of ethics. And that could result in her blowing up his life and causing a "fallout." The word "fallout," it is worth noting, was before nuclear weaponry associated with a breach of a business contract and also of friends no longer being on speaking terms. And in those contexts, the word was rather uncommon. That would all change with the dramatic Bravo incident in the Pacific in 1954 (which will be discussed in the next chapter), as the fear of radioactive fallout would from then on frame American politics and military research.[47] With the atomic bombardments of the mid-1950s, "fallout" also became a word describing unfaithful sidesteps in a relationship.

Having a "fallout" meant a breach with the "nuclear family." These nuclear analogies are worth untangling. The atomic nucleus consists of strongly bound protons, neutrinos, and energetic electrons, and the splitting of the nuclei is what releases the energy of the bomb. By analogy, the nuclear family consists of a husband, a wife, and lively kids. When the femme fatale arrives, there will be a release of sexual energy, which may result in a split of the family nuclei, followed by toxic fallout. The consequences of nuclear and sex bombs could thus both be devastating and lead to deadly fallouts.

At the time, the phrase "nuclear family" has been used in different ways. It could signify a family of bombs used in a nuclear research program, a family of nuclear allies (the United States and Britain), and finally, a family of husband, wife, and kids. The last version had different connotations. On the one hand, it signified the loss of the traditional village family, which included grandparents, aunts, uncles, and so forth. The nuclear family thus reflected a nation of immigrants common in the United States, but also families in bombed towns of Europe. As such, it was a post-war expression of loss. On the other hand, "nuclear family" was also a phrase mirrored as a seedling of a new family tree and, thus, an expression of origin and hope. Both meanings entailed a burden of expectations. "Enormous stress and great responsibilities are laid on this single bond," an anthropologist explained in 1952 because the larger family was not there anymore to support while the husband and wife also wanted to lay the ground for a promising family future. As a result, the "nuclear family" "often breaks under the strain with consequences that the number of divorces

47 Philip L. Fradkin, *Fallout: An American Nuclear Tragedy* (Tucson: The University of Arizona Press, 1989).

is increasing all the time."[48] Family fallout was a very real possibility given the sense of loss and the high expectations associated with being a nuclear family. Radiation was the antidote to the risk of a nuclear family breakup. The chief characteristic of nuclear materials (such as uranium) is radiation, and, by analogy, the nuclear family should try to be radioactive. The daily practice of "radiating love and brotherhood" (in the words of a 1948 sermon) could keep the family together.[49] What bound the family was husbands and wives practicing the art of "radiating love and confidence" toward their children.[50] With men typically providing the income, it would fall on the housewife of a nuclear family to fill the house with radiation. Radiation became a post-war image of how to energize a family with love. In 1952, a newspaper columnist typically thought a housewife should "change the atmosphere of her home by making it positively Christian, by radiating love instead of defeat."[51]

The young were to follow their parents and radiate as best as they could to be attractive on the wedding market. This was especially the case for a young woman who needed to prove that she could be a first-rate wife. If she strived at "radiating cheer" she would do well and attract a suitable man was typical advice to women at the time.[52] By the late 1950s, "a sentimental sort of radiation romance" genre in popular literature and films emerged. According to a reviewer of the material, they had a tragic "end of the world" plot—("boy does not get girl")—that typically ended with a sad "contaminated dawn" of loneliness.[53] To come within reach of both a fine-radiating woman as well as a hazardous sex bomb could complicate a young man's ability to choose. The direction of affection was an asymmetrical and existential matter. According to a 1954 issue of *Sir! A Magazine for Males*, all the nuclear radiation would "have shocking effects upon the ability of men to fall in love."[54]

---

48 Geoffrey Gorer quoted in "Western Family Life," *Sydney Le Courrier Australian*, January 31, 1952, 8. Anonymous, "Western Europe," *Braidwood Dispatch and Mining Journal*, December 17, 1953, 3.

49 Rev. Schneider, "Lenten Meditations," *Waterloo Daily Courier*, March 20, 1948, 2.

50 Inez Robb, "Last Ditch Stand," *Abilene Reporter News*, April 8, 1957, 47.

51 Dr. Spaugh, "Marriage is a Two-way Highway," *Kannapolis Daily Independent*, November 19, 1952, 4.

52 C. B. L., "Of the beat," *Provo Daily Herald*, June 12, 1960, 10.

53 Anonymous, "New Picture," *Time* 74:26 (December 28, 1959), 46.

54 Rawson Royce, "Can the H-Bomb Destroy Sex," *Sir! A Magazine for Males*, October 1954, 30–31, 58.

Riding the H-Bomb

The late 1940s and 1950s was a period in which the United States sought to come to terms with what it had done in Hiroshima and Nagasaki, as well as the increasing power of the nation's nuclear arsenal. The many nuclear analogies between nuclear weapons, women, and family life were an important part of the social process of making these weapons culturally attractive. The eroticized language of female bombshells provided an undertone of sexiness that allowed a social approval of horrific armaments. The power of female attraction nurtured a culture of nuclear acceptance.

The sexualized nuclear narrative came to its end in a tragic contaminated downfall. And it took a comedian to expose it, as famously done by Peter Sellers in *Dr. Strangelove or: How I Learned to Stop Worrying and Love the Bomb* (1964). At the end of the film, *Dr. Strangelove* (played by Sellers) successfully persuades military leaders that living in bomb shelters for over 100 years while the world recovers from nuclear Armageddon would be both pleasant and fun. To make up for the population loss, he argued, the bomb shelters protecting military and political leaders would have to be filled with sex bombs. The ratio should be "ten females to each male" and "the women will have to be selected for their sexual characteristics." The "sacrifice required" of each man would be most pleasant, Strangelove promised, and it would make the human population grow back to normal within only 20 years.[55] This sarcastic male chauvinism was not taken out of thin air but reflected instead a social culture of women and bombs being portrayed as sexy. In the final scene of the film, the hawkish commander and nuclear enthusiast Major T. J. "King" Kong sits on the bomb on its way down to Earth where it will deliver its deadly blast. He is like a joyful cowboy riding the bomb as if it's a woman. The scene captures well the dual meaning of the bomb as both destructive and erotic, and the comedy lies in exposing the ridiculous analogy.

Dr. Strangelove was the first well-known satire poking fun at the obvious and thus marks an end to naïve comparisons between nuclear explosions and a women's sexiness. At the same time, the comparisons of women to bombs would flourish over the next decades. These expressions are not innocent but

---

55 Stanley Kubrick and Peter Sellers, *Dr. Strangelove or: How I Learned to Stop Worrying and Love the Bomb*, Columbia Pictures, 1964. Jacqueline Foertsch, "Not Bombshells but Basketcases: Gendered Illness in Nuclear Texts," *Studies in the Novel* 31:4 (1999), 471–488.

nurture a culture in which women are lending erotic attractiveness to military weaponry and making destructive military practices culturally acceptable. Even the most highly educated among us tend to use these expressions uncritically, as in the case of Harvard University's erotic student magazine, *H-Bomb*.[56]

---

56 Barbara Kantrowitz, "Dropping the H Bomb: After Months of Breathless Anticipation, that School 'in Boston' Finally has its Own Sex mag. Does Anyone Care?" *Newsweek*, June 7, 2004, 45.

CHAPTER 4

PARADISE LOST

Have you ever dreamed of living in an idyllic existence under the waiving coconut palms on a remote south sea island? Of course you have. Forever since the onerous burden of civilization first began pressing its crown of thorns on romantic mankind. Who has not whispery envisioned a trip across the languid Pacific to find the tiny, lovely, lost coral island. To abandon forever the rigors of organized society. To loaf, and sleep, and fish, and swim lazily, peacefully, and happily on the bounty of a glorious tropical nature. Well, here we are on the morning of February 3, 1946, on this far-off pacific paradise [of Bikini].[1]

The official newsreel announcing the nuclear bombardment of the Bikini Atoll first aired in movie theaters on June 15, 1946. It taps into deep-seated Western imagery of life on Pacific islands. Ever since Daniel Defoe's account of *Robinson Crusoe* (1719), dreams about peaceful life on the beach have occupied Western longings along with triumphant ideas on how to civilize and suppress willing "natives" with the help of superior knowledge and technology. The images of the backward yet peaceful tropical nature in the newsreel are what allow a narrative of civilizational progress, conquest, and ultimately destruction, as the story of the nuclear bombardments of the Marshall Islands of Bikini and Enewetak runs like a Robinsonde.

---

1 Cary Wilson (narrator), "Bikini the Atom Island," Documentary, June 15, 1946. *Periscope film* archive.

The Colonization of the Enewetak and Bikini Atolls

The Second World War left the United States with the most powerful weapon, and its leaders thought the time was ripe to develop their nuclear arsenal further to empower the nation even further. By blowing up these bombs under different circumstances, the military could improve their technology, size, and power. The "Trinity" ecological disaster site in New Mexico, used for the first and only nuclear blast on U.S. soil during the war, was deemed unsuitable, as the generals wanted to see how the bombs would perform in the context of naval warfare. Besides, exploding nuclear weapons far out in the sea would minimize any risk associated with radioactive fallout. The generals decided that the Pacific atolls of Bikini and Enewetak would be ideal spots to bombard, and plans were put in place to evacuate their inhabitants.

The 167 citizens of Bikini and 140 citizens of Enewetak were no strangers to bombs, warfare, and occupations of their land. Tellingly, the Marshall Islands were not even named after one of their own, but instead after a British explorer John Marshall, who visited the islands in 1788. This was shortly after the Spanish claimed the sovereignty for the islands in 1784 as part of the Spanish East Indies. Due to colonial disputes, the islands subsequently became part of German New Guinea in 1899, which did not last long, as Japan captured them with the onslaught of the First World War in 1914 and included them in the Japanese Empire.

During these colonial regimes, the Marshallese experienced many of the ills of colonialism, including devastating diseases, forced labor, racism, resource exploitation, starvation, and so on. The Japanese military rule during the Second World War was particularly harsh with summary beheading, for example, being used as punishment for climbing trees at night to pick coconuts designated for soldiers.[2] With the U.S. Naval bombing of Japanese positions, land and villages were burned and many Marshallese lost their lives. The war had been particularly brutal at the strategic Enewetak Atoll with heavy bombardments which resulted in 30 percent of civilians killed along with the massacre of more than a thousand Japanese soldiers. At Bikini, civilians witnessed

---

2 Holly M. Barker, *Bravo for the Marshallese: Regaining Control in a Post-Nuclear, Post-Colonial World* (London: Thomson, 2004), 15–20. Serhii Plokhy, *Atoms and Ashes: A Global History of Nuclear Disasters* (New York: Norton, 2022), 1–42. Laurence Carucci, *Nuclear Nativity: Rituals of Renewal and Empowerment in the Marshall Islands* (Dekalb: Northern Illenoius University Press, 1997). Robert C. Kiste, *The Bikinians: A Study in Forced Migration* (Menlo Park: Commings Pub., 1974).

in shock their liberation, thanks to the Japanese committing collective hara-kiri. It was thus deeply shaken and fearful victims of centuries of colonization along with recent bombings that observed U.S. forces occupying their islands in 1944. After the war, the United States took control of the area through the Trust Territory of the Pacific Islands, which provided them with full adminis-trative power at the expense of local self-governance.

This backdrop may explain why the people of Enewetak and Bikini seem-ingly agreed so easily to give up their islands for nuclear bombardment. They knew firsthand that objecting to colonial rule and a military request came at a high price. Whatever bombs the military planned to use could surely not be more violent than what they had already witnessed, and they were told by Commodore Ben H. Wyatt, the military governor of the Marshalls, that they would soon be able to return. The nuclear bombardment of their islands, he explained to them echoing the *Smyth Report*, was for "the good of mankind and to end all wars" as it would create an "atomically empowered peace" for the world.[3] It is unclear if the Marshallese understood what this meant.

Years of colonialism did not hinder the Marshallese from developing and maintaining their own distinct cultures reflecting different islands and atolls located hundreds of miles apart. These cultures and their deep-seated tradi-tions moved with them when the people of Enewetak and Bikini were forcibly displaced in February 1946. Despite colonial experiences, most of them would, in looking back, express not only longing for their lost land but also life before the U.S. occupation. The people of Enewetak were resettled at Ujeland Atoll, while the Bikinians were resettled at the Rongerik Atoll, which were much smaller than their homelands. On these atolls, they would soon suffer from various struggles, starvation, and a deep sense of loss from which they would never truly recuperate.

At the Bikini Atoll, new citizens arrived immediately to prepare for "Operation Crossroads" as the nuclear detonation program was called. Some 42,000 civilian and military personnel were involved, and they brought with them 5,400 experimental rats, pigs, and goats. Most lived on over 200 naval ships, while others were on the islands. Thousands of recording devices moni-tored a bomb exploding in the air and another underwater in July 1946, with test animals suffering and dying from what humans could not endure. The bombardment was widely celebrated, with the admirals eating a large specially

---

3 Wilson, "Bikini the Atom Island," 1946.

FIGURE 4: The "Baker" Operation Crossroad destruction of the Bikini Atoll, July 1946. It was a 21-kiloton TNT bomb, slightly larger than the 15-kiloton bomb used to extinguish Hiroshima while tiny in comparison to the 15-megaton Castle Bravo obliteration in 1954. Photo: United States Department of Defense. Source: Wikimedia Commons.

designed nuclear mushroom cake in a "Salute to Bikini."[4] Similarly with a technical director on site who, upon having seen the destruction of the Atoll, concluded that "it was a very good bomb."[5]

At the Enewetak Atoll, a similar story unfolded through "Operation Sandstone," which included three bombs fired off in the spring of 1948 to research new designs of the bomb's core. The aim was not only to make them more effective but also to allow mass production. The military research was indeed successful (if that is the right word), as they allowed the Mark 4 nuclear bomb to begin rolling off the assembly line, increasing the U.S. arsenal in 1949 alone from 56 to 169 bombs. In August the same year, the Soviets blasted their first bomb in Kazakhstan. Thus, in comparing the Cold War warriors, it seems clear that the United States was the initial aggressor.

Over the next 5 years, a total of 43 bombs were detonated by the U.S. military, 12 of them at the Bikini and Enewetak atolls, while the rest were carried out at the Nevada ecological sacrifice zone. The Soviets fired off eight bombs

---

4 Anonymous, "Salute to Bikini," *Washington Post*, November 8, 1946, 18.
5 Ralph Sawyer, Task Force Technical Director at Bikini, quoted in Anonymous, "Perilous Trip Into Atom Bomb Area," *Brisbane Telegraph*, July 26, 1946, 1.

during the same period, while the British followed suit by using their first bomb in 1952 at a disaster desert site in Australia. These bombs served as evidence of national prestige in a global race of military strength between two emerging superpowers and their allies.

Both President Harry S. Truman (Democrat, 1945–1953) and President Dwight D. Eisenhower (Republican, 1953–1961) supported wholeheartedly the nuclear bombardment program. Yet there was a slight shift in policy with Eisenhower who argued that the nation should also take the lead in non-military use of nuclear power. He was feeding a widespread enthusiasm for the possibility of generating electric energy from nuclear reactors. He imagined that nuclear bombs also could be used for peaceful purposes, such as carving tunnels, harbors, and canals. Following this sentiment he warned the General Assembly at the United Nations about the "atomic danger" and made a plea for "peaceful uses of atomic energy."[6] This mixed nuclear message reflected a concern for the arms race and optimism concerning what nuclear energy could deliver for civilians. Only months after Eisenhower had addressed the UN, he approved the first use of a hydrogen nuclear weapon for military research, namely the Castle Bravo ecological annihilation of the Bikini Atoll on March 1, 1954.

The Weeping Fish

On that day, the Japanese fishing crew working on *Daigo Fukuryū Maru* (The Lucky Dragon 5) observed a strange phenomenon. They saw an odd sunrise from the west, heard incredible rumbling that engulfed the sea, and then they were covered in strange unusual white ash falling from the sky. As they later learned, they had come too close to the Castle Bravo detonation at the Bikini Atoll. Yet little did they realize the danger as they began their two-week sail back to the home port of Yaizu in Japan. They began to get headaches, diarrhea, nausea, and itchy eyes, and by the third day of their sail, as their faces turned dark, they got blisters, bodily pains, and burns, before some of their hair began to fall off. Upon their arrival in port, they went home but were eventually sent to hospital where they learned they suffered from exposure to radioactive fallout. While the doctors helped them out, most of their catch had

---

6 Dwight D. Eisenhower, "Address Before the General Assembly of the United Nations on Peaceful Uses of Atomic Energy, New York City." *U.S. Presidency Archive*, December 8, 1953, Santa Barbara.

gone to the local fish market. During the subsequent days, the fishermen's ill health became the subject of local newspaper articles, and soon, inspectors went to the fish market to examine the tuna that had yet to be auctioned off. They detected strong radiation in the remaining fish. "The fish are weeping!" they observed. From then on contaminated tuna would be known among fishermen as "the weeping fish."[7]

The story about the weeping tuna began to mushroom in the media. Who had eaten the radioactive tuna? How about other tuna for sale? The concern grew when scientists reported radiation in tuna from other boats. Public anger and fear spread when radioactive fallout from the Bravo hydrogen bomb was found in snow and rain falling over Japan in early April. The fallout contained the unknown uranium isotope U-237. Was it dangerous? Were tuna caught in the Pacific Ocean generally unsafe? Scientists continued to find contaminated fish throughout the summer and estimated that as many as twenty thousand fishermen had been exposed to radiation. With that, the public's anger and fear grew and grew, and it led to a temporary change in people's diet. Tuna fell out of favor and had to be discarded. The fish has an important status among many Japanese, so when some 457 tons of tuna had to be dumped at sea in the summer of 1954, for example, these fishermen showed sincere regrets: "the splendid big-eyed tuna, each weighing 150 pounds, turned over and over, showing their white bellies, as they sank into the sea. Watching them, the fishermen said sadly it was like sacrificing their own sons; they scattered two boxes of bait saury in the sea and joined their hands in prayer."[8] The fishermen's mourning for the loss of these tunas would continue, expressed, for example, in a commemorative plaque set up at the Tokyo fish market and a special Tuna Memorial Rock to honor fish victims.[9]

Radiation sickness and fallout were not theoretical issues for a country which less than a decade earlier had seen two of its cities decimated by nuclear bombs. It was a national trauma. The well-being of tuna, fishermen, and Japanese citizens soon evolved into a hot political topic of national concern, resulting in hectic diplomatic activity between two former enemies but now

---

7 Matashichi Ōishi, *The Day the Sun Rose in the West: Bikini, the Lucky Dragon, and I*, trans. Richard H. Minear (Honolulu: University of Hawaii Press, 2011), 29. Toshihiro Higuchi, *Political Fallout: Nuclear Weapons Testing and the Making of A Global Environmental Crisis* (Stanford: Stanford University Press, 2020), 41–60.

8 Ōishi, *The Day the Sun Rose*, 2011, 40.

9 Ōishi, *The Day the Sun Rose*, 2011, 126–133.

allied countries. The Americans tried to plant rumors about the fishermen actually being spies, but the public opinion did not buy the story. During the summer of 1954 activists managed to collect more than 30 million signatures in favor of a petition to ban nuclear weapons.[10] This is a remarkable number which illustrates the extent of the social uproar. It's surely evidence to show that the world's nuclear disarmament activism owes its origins to Japan, triggering a political process that began more formally with the first annual World Conference Against Atomic and Hydrogen Bombs that met in Hiroshima in 1955. The result of this was a political process that ultimately led to the important Partial Test Ban Treaty of 1963 which banned nuclear tests in the atmosphere.[11]

The Japanese sensed that radioactive fallout damaged not only humans but also fish and entire oceans, including its demons. The fear of radioactive fallout was depicted in the film *Godzilla*, first released in November 1954. It tells the story of a radioactive sea monster—a lucky dragon—born in the Pacific as a result of a nuclear bombing. After dramatic events in which the monster attacks and devastates Tokyo, it is eventually killed by heroic Japanese. But another monster might come back the viewers are led to believe, if nuclear bombardment continued. The subsequent series of over thirty Godzilla films came to capture the nation's nuclear trauma, depicting stories in which the Japanese take control of their own destiny.[12]

The fallout in Japan, the weeping radioactive tuna, and the faith of the fishermen did not go unnoticed in the U.S. press. Something had gone wrong and people were hurt. And in telling the news the U.S. media stayed loyal and close to whatever information the military provided. Thanks to the excellent work of the media historian, Beverly Deepe Keever, it is now known that journalists in the supposedly best newspaper, the *New York Times*, failed to ask critical questions concerning the nuclear bombings.[13] As a consequence, what

10 Nakagawa Masami, Honda Masakazu, Hirako Yoshinori, and Sadamatsu Shinjiro, "Bikini: 50 Years of Nuclear Exposure," *The Asia-Pacific Journal* 2:3 (2004), 1–5.
11 Higuchi, *Political Fallout*. Shinsuke Tomotsugu, "The Banding Conference and the Origins of Japan's Atoms for Peace Aid Program for Asian Countries," in *The Age of Hiroshima*, ed. Michale D. Gordin and G. John Ikenberry (Princeton: Princeton University Press, 2020), 109–128.
12 Nancy Anisfield, "Godzilla/Gojiro: Evolution of the Nuclear Metaphor," *Journal of Popular Culture* 29:3 (Winter 1995), 53–62.
13 Beverly Deepe Keever, *News Zero: The New York Times and the Bomb* (Monroe: Common Courage Press, 2004).

was published was filtered military propaganda stating that there had been an unfortunate incident with a Japanese fishing boat and that trustworthy military personnel and scientists were looking into the issue. The journalist George E. Herman of *CBS* may serve as an example of this. At the White House press briefing, he asked President Eisenhower in March 1954 if he would comment on "some very strong anti-American propaganda" in Japanese newspapers about radioactive poisoning, to which Eisenhower replied that "it was quite clear that this time something must have happened" and that this was one of the things his staff "was looking up."[14]

The military was indeed looking around to find out what happened, and they turned to the people and the scientists they trusted most. First among them was Ralph E. Lapp, one of the editors of the *Bulletin of Atomic Scientists*, who was sent to Japan to find out more about the tuna fishermen. His book-length report became available in bookstores and tells a story of how the military saw these events. As a scientist in the Manhattan Project and an expert in cosmic rays, he had led the group investigating the effects of the nuclear bombardment of Bikini, and his account became a semi-official popular report on what had gone wrong. It's a book laying out in great detail the fishermen's experience, while at the same time revealing very little about the bomb itself. These "Oriental fishermen were witnesses to the ultimate accomplishment of the atomic masters of the West," Lapp typically noted.[15] Lapp provides many juicy details, such as the story of how "pleasure girls" were the ones who alerted the doctors after having spent the night with fishermen. The women were wondering if the fishermen's strange symptoms were contagious.[16] Lapp provided a self-assuring narrative of the Oriental Other whose experience can be rationalized by Occidental Westerners. Yet for all its rationalisms and self-confidence, there is an underlying uncertainty in Lapp's account: how dangerous was radioactive fallout?

The Fallout on the Marshallese

The Japanese fishermen were not the only victims of the Castle Bravo bomb, which was the most powerful detonation to that date (and third largest ever)

---

14 Press briefing March 24, 1954. Ralph E. Lapp, *The Voyage of the Lucky Dragon* (London: Penguin, 1957), 114.

15 Lapp, *The Voyage of the Lucky Dragon*, 1957, 165.

16 Lapp, *The Voyage of the Lucky Dragon*, 1957, 81.

creating a 6.510 feet wide and 250 feet deep creator on the Bikini reef along with the destruction of aquatic life in the lagoon and beyond. The detonation was a new type of lithium deuteride fueled thermonuclear weapon providing the equivalent of 15 megatons of TNT blast. It did not go overly well, as it was more than twice as powerful as predicted and led to unexpected wide radioactive fallout. The mushroom cloud would rise to 130,000 feet with a 100-km radius. It was gigantic. And then the radioactive ashes began to fall to the East of Bikini. This came as no surprise to the military's weathermen who before the bomb exploded warned that the winds "were headed for Rongelap to the east" and that the atoll "would probably be contaminated."[17]

The Scientific Director of the operation, Alvin C. Graves, chose to ignore the warning, and nuclear fallout causing unspeakable human misery came as a result. He knew firsthand the dangers and suffering from radiation, having been seriously exposed to it in 1946 when he worked as the Test Director at Los Alamos. As a survivor, he had a nonchalant attitude toward radiation, and he expected the same from everyone else. When confronted about the issue he would give gibberish answers. For example, when he testified to the Joint Committee on Atomic Energy in the Congress about his decision and whether he knew radioactive fallout could cause cancer, he replied: "The danger is not that this will happen to you. The danger is that it is more likely to happen to you. Maybe the more likely is not very much more likely, but it is still more likely."[18]

Such nonsense coming from a scientist reflected partly a culture in which radiation exposure was an accepted risk, but also the fact that hazards of radioactive fallout were still poorly understood. In any case, Graves's relaxed outlook resulted in both civilians and military personnel being exposed to high levels of radioactive fallout from the Bravo detonation. The radioactive "snow" fell on several navy ships, for example, and their crews got burns and, as a result, an increased cancer rate and unspeakable suffering later in life.

Among the Marshallese, the people at Ailinginae, Rongelap, and Rongerik atolls to the East of Bikini became victims of the Bravo radioactive fallout. They received two inches of "snow" which amused them as the children played in it. The same evening they began vomiting and suffering from diarrhea,

17 Quoted in Jack Niedenthal, *For the Good of Mankind: A History of the People of Bikini and their Islands* (Majuro, MH: Bravo Book, 2013), 5.
18 Philip L. Fradkin, *Fallout: An American Nuclear Tragedy* (Tucson: The University of Arizona Press, 1989), 89–91, quote on p. 91 from a hearing in 1957.

which are typical first signs of overexposure. On these small islands, there was nowhere to go, so they were stuck in the snow. When their hair fell off they panicked, which was the state the Navy found them in when they were evacuated two days later. They had received no warning whatsoever about the detonation.

The Rongerik Atoll, it is worth recalling, was where the Bikinians had been forced to move back in 1946. After two unhappy years of starvation, most of them moved again to the Kwajalein Atoll where they lived in tents along the airstrip.[19] By the time of the Bravo detonation, most of them had resettled again at Kili Island, which lacked a lagoon and thus the traditional fishing conditions their culture and lifestyle were based on. The remaining population was 64 at Rongerik and 18 at Ailinginae in 1954, many of whom later in life would suffer from cancers due to overexposure.

Scientific Responses to the Bravo Fallout

There were mixed reactions from the scientific community, with some being uneasy while other indifferent to radioactive fallout. A manifesto written by the British philosopher Bertrand Russel, which highlighted the dangers of nuclear weapons to humanity captures the reasoning among uneasy scientists. It called for the world's scientists to intervene politically in an effort to save humankind from self-destruction. Co-signed with Albert Einstein only days before his death it in April 1955, it became known as the Russel-Einstein Manifesto. Quickly achieving the status of being the famous physicist's last word (or warning), the manifesto became widely debated and distributed. It led to the Pugwash Conferences on Science and World Affairs (after the town of Pugwash in Nova Scotia where they first met), which became a yearly event for the concerned scientists.

These skeptical scientists were the exception to the rule of scientists being mostly indifferent or positive to the use of nuclear weapons for weapons research. Radiation poisoning was a topic of concern among those working with nuclear materials before the Bravo fallout in 1954. Within the Manhattan Project, it was often framed as an issue of how long a person could be exposed to a certain dosage of radioactive material without getting sick. It was a personal issue for scientists working in direct contact with such materials, and it was researched under the rubric Health Physics, a growing field that by 1955

19 Hirshberg, *Suburban Empire,* 2022, 57–61.

had its own Health Physics Society. The focus was on human health especially the health and welfare of military personnel and scientists, while the life
and welfare of non-human species were ignored. A lengthy handbook issued in
1956 by the U.S. Department of Health on radiological toxicity, for example,
is all about radiation dosages concerning direct human exposure.[20] As both
laypeople and scientists learned about these radioactive hazards, the radioisotopes were gradually understood as environmental poisons.[21]

The same focus was also promoted by the ecologists who hardly expressed
concern for environmental radioactive degradation but instead saw ecology in
view of the human environmental well-being. The danger of radioactive materials disposed of in the environment was hardly known, nor was there a deeper
understanding of how such materials could accumulate. Two key scientists
focusing on the topic were the brothers Eugene and Howard Odum, both of
whom were supported by the Atomic Energy Commission. Eugene was a pro-
fessor at the University of Georgia with close ties to the nuclear industry. Since
the early 1950s, he had conducted ecological studies of the Savannah River
in conjunction with the site's nuclear facilities and plutonium production. He
saw radioactivity as an opportunity to investigate how materials and energy
flow within an ecosystem. With the help of radioactive tagging and a Geiger
counter, he and his team could follow, for example, how nutrients moved in
the natural environment. This approach situated him in a culture sympathetic
to everything nuclear. In collaboration with his younger brother Howard,
who was also trained in ecology, he wrote *Fundamentals of Ecology* (1953), which
quickly became the standard introduction to the field.

In lieu of the Bravo fallout, the Atomic Energy Commission asked the
Odum brothers if they could carry out ecological research at the Enewetak
Atoll to find out more about radioactive fallout from the detonation. As a result,
they spent six weeks in the summer of 1954 at the marine research station there
to study its reef ecosystem. They focused on the Japtan reef which they describe
as "a relatively undisturbed and fairly typical inter-island reef" and as a "reef,
which has not yet been directly disturbed by nuclear explosions" even though

---

20 Simon Kinsman, *Radiological Health Handbook* (Cincinnati: U.S. Department of Health,
Educaton and Welfare, 1956).
21 Angeka N. H. Creager, *Life Atomic: A History of Radioisotopes in Science and Medicine*
(Chicago: University of Chicago Press, 2013).

"algae on the dead reef surfaces were intensely radioactive."[22] To describe the reef as "relatively undisturbed" is remarkable given the fact that there had been altogether ten nuclear explosions on the atoll before their arrival, with the closest being only nine miles away (at Runit Island in 1948 and 1951) and the largest being Ivy Mike, a ten megaton explosion twenty miles away that obliterated the large Elugaleb Island in 1952 (five hundred times the yield of the bomb that annihilated Nagasaki). The latest detonation took place in mid-May 1954, about six weeks before the Odum brothers arrived, off the Bogon Islet near the Ivy Mike crater in late June. It was a large 1.69 megaton bomb that was detonated submerged and thus decimated coral reefs and aquatic life in the lagoon and beyond. Their description of the intensely blasted reef as "relatively undisturbed" is scientifically questionable, to say the least.[23]

Yet having established that the reef was "relatively undisturbed" the Odum brothers could argue that it should "serve as a 'control' for studies of reefs more directly affected by nuclear weapons tests."[24] The reef they observed was to them a harmonious "steady state community" in a "balance of growth and decay" and an example of "a true ecological climax" from which humans should learn: "for mankind's great civilization is not in steady state and its relation with nature seems to fluctuate erratically and dangerously."[25] Thus, the Japtan reef was not only to serve as a clean gold standard for how the measure reefs were truly affected by nuclear explosions but also as a model for a more harmonious human civilization. Whatever dreams of "a steady state" humanity the Odums had, the ecologists did not respond to it. Instead, it was functional (as opposed to a structural approach) to ecosystems that made their Enewetak reef study famous. When published in 1955 it became one of

22 Eugene T. Odum and Howard P. Odum, "Trophic Structure and Productivity of a Windward Coral Reef Community on Eniwetok Atoll," *Ecological Monographs* 25:3 (July 1955), 291–320, quotes on p. 293, 301, 318. Emory Jerry Jessee, *Radiation Ecologies: Bombs, Bodies and Environment During the Atmospheric Nuclear Weapons Testing Period*, Ph.D. thesis (Bozeman: Montana State University, 2013), 234–249. Laura J. Martin, "Proving Grounds: Ecological Fieldwork in the Pacific and the Materialization of Ecosystems," *Environmental History* 23 (2018), 567–592.
23 Todd A. Hanson, "Expendable Enewetak: An Environmental History of a Cold War Islandscape," in *Entire of Itself? Towards an Environmental History of Islands*, ed. Milica Prokić and Pavla Šimková (Winwick: White Horse Press, 2024), 191–214.
24 Eugene T. Odum and Howard P. Odum, "Zonation of Corals on Japtan Reef, Eniwetok Atoll," *Atoll Research Bulletin* 52 (1957), 1–4, quote p. 1.
25 Odum and Odum, "Trophic Structure," 1955, 291, 304, 318, 319.

the Odum brothers' most widely cited papers. For all the fame, it was still an intramural paper that received little notice outside the closed community of ecologists.

What seems clear is that the reef study resulted exactly in what the Odum brothers' patron, the Atomic Energy Commission, wanted to hear, namely, that there was only minuscule environmental damage on oceanic life due to radiation at Enewetak. Their research gave evidence to show that nuclear bombs did little or no harm and that it was safe to continue with the subsequent ecological destruction of the atoll. This was carried out in 1956 and 1958 with the help of 33 nuclear detonations. With the final blast in 1958 altogether 43 bombs with a combined yield of 38.8 megatons had been detonated at the tiny atoll.

To address the Japanese concern for contaminated tuna, the Atomic Energy Commission began investigating the damaging effects of radioactivity on oceans. This resulted in a daunting report from the National Academy of Sciences entitled *The Effects of Atomic Radiation on Oceanography and Fisheries* (1957). Its conclusion was most reassuring: "Tests of atomic weapons can be carried out over or in the sea," it stated, and with the coming of nuclear energy it was also "convenient and perhaps necessary to dispose of some of these [nuclear] industrials wastes in the oceans." Most importantly, it was paramount to battle the public's "ignorance and emotionalism" with respect to radioactive fallout and instead put trust in (and provide more funding for) the Academy.[26] These broad conclusions, which must have pleased the nuclear-friendly military and politicians alike, were based on more detailed reports by scientists from different fields of study, including one from the ecologists.[27] The collection was typically reviewed as "stimulating and authoritative articles" settling the public's concern concerning fallout.[28]

---

26 Roger Revelle and Milner B. Shaefer, "General considerations," in *The Effects of Atomic Radiation on Oceanography and Fisheries* (Washington: National Academy of Sciences, 1957), 1–25, quote p. 23. Jacob Hamblin, *Poison in the Well* (New Brunswick: Rutgers University Press, 2008).

27 Louis A. Krumholz and Edward D. Goldberg, "Ecological Factors Involved in the Uptake, Accumulation, and Loss of Radionuclides by Aquatic Organisms," in *The Effects of Atomic Radiation on Oceanography and Fisheries* (Washington: National Academy of Sciences, 1957), 69–79.

28 G. F. Humphrey, "The Effects of Atomic Radiation on Oceanography and Fisheries" (review), *Science* 128:3326 (September 26, 1958), 709.

With the scientists in general and ecologists, in particular, having proved that nuclear fallout did little or no harm to Pacific environments, the road was open for further bombardments of Pacific atolls, ocean waters, and its people. The only thing to worry about was the direct fallout on human beings, as pointed out by the Health Physics community. As a result, the military continued blasting the Bikini Atoll with 23 new bombs, decimating the atoll between 1954 and 1958. All in all, the United States carried out hundred and five detonations in the Pacific, including at sites not discussed here, such as the Kiritimati Island and the Kalama Atoll in addition to bombs detonated in the open ocean, with a total yield of about 210 megatons.

For the Good of Mankind?

About 10 years later, in 1967, the Atomic Energy Commission welcomed the Bikinians back to their homeland. It was safe to return to the Bikini Atoll, they were told. Over the next years, they were gradually resettled as crops were planted, buildings rebuilt, and radioactive materials cleaned up. Family by family the Bikinis moved back and began restoring their life until 1975, when it was discovered that both their food and drinking water were seriously contaminated. In September 1979, after some new studies, the Bikinians were once again forced to leave their atoll.

It had since been possible to visit the atoll, but only for a short-term stay. Being there for long entails too much radioactive exposure. A reporter visiting in 1997, for example, noted that the atoll was "an atomic age Eden (but don't eat the coconuts)" due to them being radioactive.[29] With minimal human interference animals and plants had begun to prosper on the islands, although little is known about what damage, suffering, or pain radioactivity is doing to them. As a result, both Bikini and Enewetak have become wilderness atolls of some sort, and what human activity does exist relates to nuclear ecotourism and scuba diving to the sunken navy ships. Yet it's impossible to imagine a future there reflecting how Marshallese people once lived with the environment, making the atolls for human waste.

On Friday, September 3, 2010, UNESCO approved a resolution to include the Bikini Atoll among the World Heritage sites. It was triggered by a lengthy

---

29 Nicolas D. Kristof, "An Atomic Age Eden (but Don't Eat the Coconuts)," *New York Times*, March 5, 1997. Peter Galison, "Westland and Wilderness," lecture given in different versions since about 1997.

nomination from the Republic of the Marshall Islands. The Senator for the People of Bikini, Tomaki Juda, wrote a moving statement of support in which he argued for protecting the atoll's nuclear heritage. The Bikini Atoll had played a major role in nuclear history, he argued, and could as a heritage site remind people about the importance of making the world a more peaceful place. We "will always feel pain for what we have lost," he noted, but perhaps it, in the end, would result in "global peace and the elimination of weapons of mass destruction." In making his case, he quoted the arguments Commodore Wyatt made to his father back in 1946 for why the Bikinians had to move due to nuclear bombardments. It was "for the good of mankind and to end all world wars."[30] Indeed, the quote—which echoed White House propaganda from 1945—was on the front page of the World Heritage application. The reasoning for how to best manage the atoll today is thus still that of the colonizer, and the Bikinians are still submitting to the will and narrative of the U.S. military. What was once propaganda to lure them into leaving their homes has now become their official legacy, their way of making sense of history. The title of the book of their chief historian, *For the Good of Mankind: A History of the People of Bikini and Their Islands*, captures the sense in which the Bikinis now express pride in knowing that their islands were turned into ecological sacrifice zones in the name of weapons research.[31]

Thankfully, Marshallese islanders are no longer facing the prospect of nuclear bombardments. Instead, a new kind of existential threat has emerged in the shape of raising seawater. Their vulnerability to global warming has a deeper history reaching back to how concerned citizens questioning nuclear power provoked scientific questions about anthropogenic climate change. All of which will be the topic of the next chapter.

---

30 Kili-Bikini-Ejit Local Government, *Bikini Atoll Nomination* (Majuro: Republic of the Marshall Islands, 2009), 1 and 7. "War Department Release on New Mexico Test," *Atomic Archive,* July 16, 1945. Smyth, *Smyth Report*, 1945, 247.
31 Niedenthal, *For the Good of Mankind*, 2013.

CHAPTER 5

THE CLIMATE BOMB

In November 1946, the *New York Herald Tribune* reported some alarming news. Scientists had discovered a global trend of warmer weather in the form of "a climatic change affecting the entire earth." The cause of the warming was "shrouded in mystery," although the journalist reported that it was likely due to the heat generated by the rapid disintegration of radium. The "rising temperature of all four seasons" was caused by an "explosive phenomenon" of "atomic reactions," which made a substantial contribution to the earth's temperature.[1]

This was not the first time scientists noticed a long-term trend of warmer weather. Upward leading temperature curves had been published in meteorological journals for at least a decade. An article from 1933, for example, compares long-term rise in temperature at different locations in the northern and southern hemispheres.[2] And lay leaders learned that "Maybe Grandpa was Right about Colder Weather" back in May 1945.[3] What is noticeable about the *Herald Tribune* article is that the warmer weather was explained as a result of nuclear explosions.

Climatic change had previously been explained by natural phenomena such as meteorological weather cycles, movements in the Earth's crust, and fluctuations in the energy from the sun, or also extraordinary natural events

---

1 John O. Neill, "Trend to Warmer Weather," *New York Herald Tribune,* November 10, 1946, A10. Inspired by J. B. Kincer, "Our Changing Climate," *Transactions, American Geophysical Union* 27:3 (June 1946), 342–347. Kincer does not provide a cause for climatic change.

2 Joseph B. Kincer, "Is Our Climate Changing? A Study in Long Term Temperature Trends," *Monthly Weather Review* 61:9 (September 1933), 251–259.

3 Max Hall, "Maybe Grandpa was Right about Colder Weather," *Findlay Republican Courier,* May 17, 1945, 6. Similarly in Max Hall, "Winters Not so Cold," *Lincoln Nebraska State Journal,* May 12, 1945, 5.

such as the eruptions of volcanoes. That climate change could be caused by radioactivity reflected something new, namely the arrival of the all-powerful nuclear bomb. It was an explanation that, on the face of it, made sense. After all, how could huge powerful bombs not affect climate? As it turned out, the warming weather was not caused by nuclear bombs but by another invisible and silent agent: carbon dioxide generated by the burning of fossil fuels. The explanation appealed to the public because carbon dioxide, just like radioactive clouds, was a dangerous invisible agent that could not be detected visually or through smell. Moreover, what the bomb did for climate debates was to open up the possibility of human agency being a key factor for warming weather.

Climate Engineering

Could the heavens be set on fire by a nuclear bomb? Arthur Compton, a Nobel-winning physicist who worked for the Manhattan Project, contemplated the question in all sincerity while designing the bomb during the war. It was a chemical reaction in the air's nitrogen triggered by extreme heat he feared. Perhaps all the nitrogen in the air could be "set off by an atomic explosion in the atmosphere?"[4] After some scrutiny and calculations he concluded that the chance was miniscule, and by the time of the Trinity detonation in July 1945 that turned the beautiful White Sands near Alamogordo into an ecological disaster site, he joked about it to his colleagues by saying: "Now, let's make a bet whether the atmosphere will be set on fire by this test."[5]

While the atmosphere was obviously not set on fire, it is worth reflecting on the hubris of the bet even if it was meant innocently and the probability was miniscule. It illustrates that the imagined and real power of the nuclear weapon reached beyond the Earth. With the bomb, scientists contemplated having the power to change, perhaps even destroy, the very atmosphere in which we live.

With the end of the war, there was no shortage of such confidence with respect to what humans could do with the newfound nuclear power. "When can the atom be put to work?" was the title of a *New York Times* article reflecting the mood of the period. The journalist imagined that nuclear energy could be important also in peacetime, providing energy for factories and homes, even

---

4 P. S. Buck, "The Bomb - The End of the World?" *The American Weekly*, Mars 8, 1959, 8–9, 14.

5 Quoted in John Horgan, "Bethe, Teller, Trinity and the End of the Earth," *Scientific American*, August 4, 2005, online.

in the Arctic. It was also suggested the bomb could help excavating a larger Panama Canal and also "improve the climate of Sahara Desert" by blasting new fjords into northern Africa and thereby letting in the waters of the Mediterranean Sea.[6] The global (some would say imperial) aspirations for what the United States could do with nuclear energy were blatant, with the bombs being put to work well outside national borders. This newfound optimism is also apparent in a speech President Harry Truman gave in Congress in 1945 saying that nuclear energy "may someday prove to be more revolutionary to human society than the invention of the wheel."[7]

It is buried in this self-confidence on behalf of newly discovered nuclear energy that the turn toward the sentiment that humans (and not nature) could be the cause of global warming. From the very beginning of the Cold War, the atmosphere became an arena for national security and control. After all, bomb-carrying rockets travel in the atmosphere. And weather forecasting was tightly tied to such military technology, with V2 rockets enabling high-altitude research.[8] With the atmosphere being of keen military interest, the idea also emerged of manipulating it to gain a martial advantage. The historian of science James R. Fleming has reviewed this endeavor in some detail, and he shows that military as well as private interests put significant efforts into weather and climate engineering in the post-war period.[9] For private entrepreneurs it was all about creating artificial rain for farmers, and perhaps also some sun for vacationers annoyed with gray weather at their beach resorts. For the military, climate engineering could generate cloud cover for advancing troops, and also be a weapon against civilians by halting food production as a result of hindering rain on enemy territory. The physicist Edward Teller, for example, told a Senate military committee to "please imagine a world in which the Russians can control weather in a big scale [so that they can] influence the rainfall in our country in an adverse manner."[10] In view of this, it was urgent that the U.S.

---

6 Harry M. Davis, "When Can the Atom Be Put to Work?" *New York Times*, December 9, 1945, 90. Edward Teller, et al., *The Constructive Use of Nuclear Weapons* (New York: McGraw-Hill, 1968).

7 Quoted in Davis, "When Can the Atom Be Put to Work?" 1945, 90.

8 D. D. Clark, "High Altitude Research with Rockets," *Weather* 4 (1949), 176–182.

9 James R. Fleming, *Fixing the Sky: The Checkered History of Weather and Climate Control* (New York: Columbia University Press, 2010).

10 Edward Teller to the Senate Military Preparedness Subcommittee, November 1957. Quoted in Clinton P. Anderson, "Toward Greater Control," in *Science and Resources*, ed. Henry Jarrett (Baltimore: John Hopkins Press, 1959), 54–62, quote pp. 60–61.

military advanced climate engineering technologies, he argued. Such military and civilian aims could be achieved, according to the proponents, by seeding the clouds with dry ice from airplanes or also by shooting iodized silver into the clouds from the ground.

Such climate engineering was a hot topic in the late 1940s and throughout the 1950s. The sun- and rain-makers imagined their future powers as so real that Congress initiated laws to regulate the activity. It could have legal consequences if rain-makers accidentally created a shower on a sunbathing resort or on farmland in need of the sun. It was in this context the U.S. Weather Bureau in 1946 got its own Section of Industrial Climatology to deal with the commodification of climate.[11] And within the next decade, an official Advisory Committee on Weather Control suggested legal and political frameworks for the weather. Climate engineering was not perceived a nutty fantasy, but imagined as a serious business in need of federal control and legislation. For example, in 1950, fifty pounds of silver iodide was being put into the air per week in order to generate rain in the dry state of New Mexico but it resulted instead in unintentional heavy rainfall on the East Coast. People on all sides were upset with the failure of the rain-makers, and Congress saw the need to regulate the business. Officials wanted more control over climate engineers, as weathering technologies also were of military interest. Perhaps the United States needed "a federal czar for weather?"[12] Both the Congress and the White House were involved in such legislation well into the 1950s.

It's a truism that people care about the weather. As a result, climate engineering generated intense enthusiasm, blame games, and public rage whenever the weather was not according to the liking.[13] Human weather control received much press and became part of the public imagination, and all the attention nurtured the thought among lay people that human agency actually could change the atmosphere.

11 Helmut Landsberg, "Climate as a Natural Resource," *The Scientific Monthly* 63:4 (October 1946), 293–298.
12 Anonymous, "A Federal Czar for Weather," *U.S. News and World Report* 30:13 (March 30, 1951), 22–23. *Advisory Committee on Weather Control, Final Report*, Washington, 1958.
13 Anonymous, "About Policing Rainmakers," *U.S. News and World Report* 35:10 (September 4, 1953), 67.

"Go North, Young Man"

While the climate engineers were nurturing a culture of commodification, control, and manipulation of weather, the climate got warmer. In the late 1940s, newspapers and academic journals wrote avidly about the phenomena. "Signs are multiplying that the climate of the world's Northern Hemisphere, and perhaps the whole earth, is becoming warmer," a Canadian news reporter noted in 1947, for example. It meant that the great Canadian forests would be growing north and that agriculture would be possible in the subarctic zone, but also that the nation's many glaciers would melt, resulting in rising oceans that could inundate coastal settlements. As a consequence, the warming climate was "one of the most important factors in the life of mankind."[14] A similar article in the *New York Times* from 1947 warned its reader that the rapid melting of glaciers should worry people living by the ocean's shorelines.[15]

The warming weather trend continued with sweltering heat in the summer of 1950. An article published in the July issue of *Life* claimed that "the climate is changing." The "north polar icecap has been retreating" and Americans should brace for a rise in the ocean level of "at least 90 feet, causing a dislocation of property values in such shore settlements as New York City, San Francisco and New Orleans."[16] The reason for the changing climate was unknown. "Mysterious changes are occurring in the atmosphere" and "the planet as a whole is warming gradually," a journalist noted. The Horace Greeley of the future would say: "Go north, young man," instead of "Go west," as climatic changes soon would open northern lands as a new frontier. "Baffinland will be as warm as Minnesota, Greenland as warm as the Carolinas, Vladivostok as warm as Calcutta," the readers of the *Saturday Evening Post* were told. As a consequence, deserts would grow in the south while new agricultural land would emerge in the north, and millions of people would have to migrate toward the

14 Gladwin Hill, "Forecast: Warmer," *Maclean's Magazine* 60:24 (December 15, 1947), 12–58. Following the Swedish scientist. Dr. Hans Ahlmann of Stockholm University's Geographical Institute.
15 Gladwin Hill, "Warming Arctic Climate Melting Glaciers Faster, Raising Ocean Level, Scientist Says," *New York Times,* May 30, 1947, 23.
16 Robert Coughlan, "That Infernal Weather," *Life* 29:5 (July 31, 1950), 74–81.

poles.[17] The changing habits of birds and mammals were a further source of concern as it also demonstrated that the world was getting warmer.[18]

Those in favor of climate engineering could not explain the general trend toward warmer weather. Rain-making, all parties agreed, was more or less a local enterprise. George H. T. Kimble, the Director of the Metrological Observatory at McGill University, speculated that a "change of the climate" has been caused by "some change in the Golf Stream or in the warm air masses that originate in the Gulf of Mexico region."[19] Whatever the cause, he argued, the climate engineers could take care of it and provide the ideal weather if the public just provided the funds.[20]

The changing climate also opened up an interest in a deeper understanding of environmental history. One of the proponents was the ecologist, Paul Sears, who saw recent trends of warmer weather in lieu of climate history reaching back millennia. In 1952 he told members of the American Association for the Advancement of Science that his botanical discoveries confirmed that the climate of North America was "continually getting warmer and drier," a trend he "expected to continue several centuries."[21] His report was among the most significant of some two hundred papers presented at the convention, which attracted more than five thousand scientists. Sears had investigated fossil tree pollen preserved below the surface of dried-up lake beds in the Southwest and compared these to more recent layers of pollen. The trend he found was troubling. He concluded that we may "anticipate a continuation of the climate change" and should, as a consequence, focus on bettering our environmental management, especially with respect to water.[22]

17 Albert Abarbanel and Thorp McClusky, "Is the World Getting Warmer?" *Saturday Evening Post,* July 1, 1950, 22, 57, 60–63.

18 Anonymous, "Is Climate Changing? Habits of Mammals and Birds Suggest World Is Warmer," *New York Times,* October 15, 1950, E9.

19 Anonymous, "Retreat of the Cold," *Time* 58:18 (October 29, 1951), 78.

20 George H. T. Kimble, "The Changing Climate," *Scientific American* 182:4 (April 1950), 48–53.

21 Anonymous, "Climate Change in U.S. Threaten Water Scarcity," *St. Petersburg Times,* December 28, 1952, 10D. Paul B. Sears, "Climate and Civilization," in *Climatic Change: Evidence, Causes, and Effects,* ed. H. Shapley (Cambridge: Harvard University Press, 1953), 35–50.

22 Anonymous, "Will climate of U.S. turn too warm, dry?" *Lincoln Sunday Journal and Star,* December 27, 1952, 1.

The climate of the Arctic became a focal point in the accounts of the warming weather. Alaska, Greenland, Canada, and Spitsbergen, it is worth recalling, were at the very forefront of the Cold War against the Soviets. Washington's Arctic Institute was a chief government-sponsored organization that mobilized interest and knowledge designed to keep the public aware of the northern region's strategic importance. "It is high time" that the world notes that "the climate of the Arctic has been warming up," its director argued in 1954.[23] Its changing weather "may eventually make the barren lands flow with milk and honey."[24] Such blatant optimism was not the mission of the Institute, but just a way of drawing the public's attention to the region. Images of melting glaciers and rising oceans could also serve the purpose.

The cause of the rising temperature was perfectly unclear, which opened the door wide for both scientific and public speculation. Could the cause of climatic change be the cycles of mountain building and degradation? Or perhaps it was caused by the variations in the eccentricity of the earth's orbit? Minor changes in the distribution of land and water could also be the cause, or perhaps it was due to long-period variations in solar activity. The passing of the earth through cosmic dust, the wobbling of the earth's poles, and the almost imperceptible drifting of the continents were also candidates for explaining why the globe was getting warmer.[25] These were all arguments pointing to natural events beyond human control. Then there were also two competing explanations for global climatic change which blamed human agency: nuclear bombs and carbon dioxide. Of the two of them the nuclear, at least initially, sounded most probable and got the most attention.

Climate Change and Nuclear Bombs

For the wider public, the answer was clear. Nuclear bombs were to blame not only for warmer weather but also for any kind of abnormal weather. And the meteorologists did their best to point out that they were not aware of any direct causal link between bombs and the weather experienced. "Yet the letters and telephone calls from worried citizens clog the Weather Bureau switchboard," blaming nuclear bombardments for warmer weather, a meteorologist complained as early as 1948. One frustrated forecaster, James W. Osmun,

---

23 Anonymous, "Warmer Future," *Time* 64:4 (July 26, 1954), 42.
24 Anonymous, "Too warm for birches," *Time* 64:20 (November 15, 1954), 69.
25 Anonymous, "Globe Getting Warmer," *Anniston Star*, October 11, 1951, 4.

explained that the weather does not change due to nuclear explosions. Blaming the bomb was, to him, simply "Poppycock!"[26]

Yet, the idea of nuclear bombs being the cause of climatic change persisted. During the heat wave and other assorted meteorological novelties that swept the United States in the summer of 1950, the popular lay explanation was that it was all due to the atmosphere having been poisoned by radioactive fallout.[27] The scientists continued to reject that idea, with officials at the Weather Bureau blaming climatic change on natural (and not human) forces, such as a slow increase in radiation from the sun.[28] Such announcements did not settle the matter, as concerned citizens continued to point to the bomb as the source of all strange things to do with the climate. During the warm summer of 1951, for example, the weather forecasters would have to issue another strong rejection arguing that climate change could not be traced back to human activity, such as atom bombs and rain-makers.[29]

The connection between nuclear blasts and changing weather was particularly important to those living in the proximity of the Nevada disaster site. Many citizens of Los Angeles were sure there was some sort of connection and would make their voices heard by the local meteorologists. The meteorologists in turn, again and again, had to go out and inform the public about the spurious connection. "Any effects of A-bomb explosions have on the weather are limited to the immediate locality of the blasts," was a typical response.[30] And nuclear energy officials had to go out and publically deny that they had been tampering with the weather: "All those snowstorms in the West [...] were caused by nature, not neutrons."[31] Yet that did not settle the matter as nuclear energy officials were known to keep things secret, and the public would continue to ask weather officials about what role nuclear bombardments in

---

26 Meyer Berger, "Weepy Weather Entirely Normal, Temperature, Too, Expert Insists," *New York Times,* June 15, 1948, 29.

27 Coughlan, "That Infernal Weather."

28 Anonymous, "Getting Warmer?" *Time,* May 15, 1950, 76–77.

29 Jerome Namias, "No, the Weather Isn't Changing: It's just Behaving Crazily, as Usual," *New York Times,* October 21, 1951, 170.

30 William S. Barton, "Weather Expert Finds Little Climate Change," *Los Angeles Times,* June 16, 1952, 12.

31 Anonymous, "'Puny' Atom Is Defended As Nevada Storm Villain," *New York Times,* March 29, 1952, 7.

Nevada played in causing any abnormal weather. The patient meteorologist on duty had to over and over again reply that the answer was none.[32]

The concerned citizens had a point. The meteorology experts did not have a full overview concerning what a huge nuclear detonation could do to the atmosphere. The nuclear scientists were not known to share their secrets, and large explosions in the past had caused a change in the global climate. An angry letter to the *New York Times* pointed out that a volcanic eruption, such as the Tambora eruption in 1815, which led to a "year without summer" in 1816, could be compared to a large nuclear detonation. Nuclear "dusts hurl[ed] high and wide may exert a 'trigger effect' on weather conditions because of nucleation."[33]

The public worry grew into a political concern, and by 1953 Congressman Ray J. Madden of Indiana called for a thorough investigation of the relationship between nuclear bombing in Nevada and the unusual number of tornados that had plagued the state of Indiana. "The public is entitled to know if there is any connection between the A-bomb explosions and the tornados which have followed," he proclaimed. We know that radioactive "material pollutes the air we breathe and the water we drink. Does it also generate abnormal atmospheric conditions?" he asked.[34] As a result, researchers had to address the issue head-on by providing a thorough scientific answer.

The result came in a review article published in 1955 in the prestigious journal *Nature*, which once and for all was supposed to settle the matter. It was signed by Graham Sutton, the Director of the British Meteorological Office, who in that capacity could be seen as a neutral observer not connected to anything nuclear in the United States.[35] His conclusion was clear: there was no connection between thermonuclear explosions and the weather, except, perhaps, at the disaster site itself. The bomb did generate a minor (radioactive) cloud. And that was about it. The result of his report was widely distributed in the press with journalists pointing out that nuclear explosions did not cause freakish weather, blizzards, rain, tornadoes, lightning, or drought. "When the best available observational evidence and the most plausible theories are

---

32 Anonymous, "Bomb Tests Are Cleared As Cause of Rain in East," *New York Times*, May 22, 1953, 3.

33 Jerome Alexander, "A-Bomb Effects on Weather," *New York Times*, May 28, 1953, 22.

34 Anonymous, "Inquiry on Atom Effects Asked," *New York Times*, June 10, 1953, 40.

35 Graham Sutton, "Thermonuclear Explosions and the Weather," *Nature* 4451 (February 1955), 319–321.

considered together, there appears to be no reason for believing that any past nuclear bombardments at the Nevada Proving Grounds has had any significant effect on the weather more than a few miles from the test site," a journalist typically concluded.[36]

It was not only in the United States that such speculations about changing climate and bombs can be found. For the Parisians, 1951 had been a particularly wet summer, with record-breaking rain. And they were wondering why. A French communist journal promoting the Soviets used the opportunity to expound the theory that the bad weather was the direct result of U.S. nuclear bombardments of Pacific atolls, thereby feeding the French anti–United States sentiment. The "thunderous storms which are devastating our crops and raising even higher the market price of cherries and salads,"[37] the communists claimed, were somehow connected to "the American experiments at Eniwetok Atoll." This critical sentiment can also be found in Japan where weather experts argued that particle dusts from hydrogen bombing in the Pacific in 1954 behaved similarly to volcanic eruptions and that they could bring about climatic change in the form of "a drastic drop in temperature which could cause frost damage to crops."[38]

Such worries connecting nuclear bombs and fallout with climatic change would continue at least until the end of the 1950s. "No matter what the meteorologists may say, the belief persists in America and Europe that what are regarded as 'peculiarities' of the weather are caused by explosions of the atomic bombs," the *New York Times* reported.[39] Although the public imagination of what nuclear bombs could do to the weather turned out to be mistaken, it prepared their minds to accept that humans could cause climate change on a global scale. This is the key legacy of nuclear bombs in the climate debate. If nuclear detonation did not cause warmer weather, what did? As an alternative scientifically approved explanation, human emissions of carbon dioxide emerged as a better candidate to blame for the warming weather. Just like radioactive clouds, the gas was a silent invisible agent of destruction.

36 Anonymous, "Weather Bad? Don't Blame the Atom," *U.S. News and World Report*, March 4, 1955, 32.

37 Anonymous, "Weather or Not," *Time* 58:2 (September 7, 1951), 25.

38 Anonymous, "Jap Weather Expert Tells of Bomb Effects: Climatic Change May Follow Blast," *Camden News*, April 23, 1954, 1. Also in *Petersburg Progress*, April 23, 1954, 1, 6. Argument by Hidetoshi Araki.

39 Anonymous, "Bombs and Weather: Last Summer's Explosions Had No Discernible Effects," *New York Times*, March 20, 1955, E11.

The Invisible Blanket

The idea that human emissions of carbon dioxide may affect climate has been around for a while, with scientific and newspaper articles written about the possibility reaching back to the end of the nineteenth century.[40] Yet these were rare and framed as only theoretical possibilities, or also not taken entirely seriously. What would change in the early 1950s was the frequency of articles about and also the sincerity of reports of carbon dioxide emissions being the candidate explaining global warming. What catalyzed and propelled these publications was the public's demand for an alternative explanation of warming weather to blaming nuclear bombs.

In October 1949, *Boston Globe* published what may have been the first postwar article about human carbon dioxide emissions from the burning of coal and oil causing "world-wide warmer weather."[41] In retrospect, one could only wish, of course, that the article had been mailed as a personal perfumed love letter to every citizen in the world. But that did not happen. It was quickly buried in other news, and then forgotten or overseen – even by savvy historians of climate change science. What triggered the report was a scientific article by the British researcher Guy S. Callendar, asking "Can Carbon Dioxide Influence Climate?" His answer was yes. The "changes brought about by human agency," he argued, can indeed disturb the carbon balance of the earth and cause a long trend of warmer weather.[42] Today his article is hailed as a milestone. And rightly so. At the time it was received as a competing theory to those who blamed warming weather on natural phenomena. The winter of 1950 was unusually warm, especially on the U.S. East Coast, and the local meteorologists were called upon to explain the phenomena.[43] They juxtaposed

40 Roland Jackson, *The Ascent of John Tyndall* (Oxford: Oxford University Press, 2018). James Rodger Fleming, *The Callendar Effect* (Boston: American Meteorological Society, 2007). Spencer R. Weart, *The Discovery of Global Warming* (Cambridge, MA: Harvard University Press, 2008).
41 Pat Munroe, "Humans May Have Created Worldwide Warm Weather," *Daily Boston Globe,* October 23, 1949, 7. Also published in *Lincoln Sunday Journal and Star,* October 23, 1949, 10.
42 Guy S. Callendar, "Can Carbon Dioxide Influence Climate?" *Weather* 4 (1949), 310–314.
43 Rowland Evan, "Weather Forecasters Amazed at Abnormal Conditions," *Greeley Daily Tribune,* January 16, 1950, 13; "Look Out! Winter is Not Over," *Sedalia Democrat,* January 14, 1950, 13; "Weatherman, Rarely Surprised are Really up a Stump: Why is it so Warm, they Ask," *Independent Record,* January 14, 1950, 2; "Mild Eastern Winter

two competing explanations, namely Callendar's conclusion and the explanation put forward by Swedish glaciologist Wilson Ahlmann, who thought that
the warm winter was due to an increasing amount of warmer "maritime air"
drifting inland. Ahlmann's account of warm weather reflected mainstream
meteorology, while Callendar's theory represented a more daring explanation
pointing to human agency.

Reporters would, in subsequent years, continue to compare the carbon
dioxide emissions to natural causes for climatic change, although gradually
also begin contrasting it to those who claimed nuclear bombs were behind
the warming. In these comparisons, the nuclear bomb's explanation was often
portrayed as the silly ignorant one, especially in contrast to Callendar's sturdy
scientific account. In the unusually hot summer of 1950, for example, a housewife in Boston was quoted saying: "It's those atom bombs [...] they've blown
holes in the sky, and the sun is going to burn us all to cinders." Against this
backdrop of ignorance, Callendar was introduced to the reader with a more
sober explanation of how carbon dioxide emissions from the burning of coal
and oil prevented heat from escaping the atmosphere.[44]

By 1953, the "Invisible Blanket" of carbon dioxide in the atmosphere was
no longer a speculative theory, but looking more like a fact. If "industrial
growth continues, the earth's climate will continue to grow warmer," an article in *Time* concluded.[45] It was the Johns Hopkins Physicist Gilbert N. Plass,
who went public with a warning against burning more coal and oil as the speed
by which humans were doing so would raise the earth's temperature by at
least 1.5° Fahrenheit every 100 years, leading to less rain and an overall drier
climate. The *Time* article was published in May during the hottest spring on

Amazes Metrologists," *Florence Morning News*, January 22, 1950, 3. Anonymous, "Look
Out! Winter Not Over Yet," *Zanesville Signal*, January 14, 1950, 32; "White Heat: Weather
Experts Frankly Amazed at the Unusually Mild Weather," *Detroit Free Press*, January 15,
1950, 1; "Weather Men Amazed," *Pittsfield Berkshire Evening Eagle*, January 15, 1950. 2;
"Weather Forecasters Say High Temperatures to Stay," *Waterloo Daily Courier*, January
14, 1950, 22; "Oldtimers Say Winters Milder than Formerly – They're Right," *Kaufman
Herald*, February 1, 1950, 4. M. G. Fitzpatrick, "Becoming Warmer?" (Editorial), *Olean
Times Herald*, January 19, 1950, 20.

44 Jhan Robbins and June Robbins, "Forecast ... Hotter and Hotter," *New York Herald
Tribune*, June 11, 1950, F11.

45 Anonymous, "Invisible Blanket," *Time*, May 25, 1953, 82–83. Similarly in Anonymous,
"The Earth is a Hothouse," *Scientific American* 189:1 (July 1953), 44, 46; "Swirls in Earth's
Core," *The Science News-Letter* 63:20 (May 16, 1953), 307.

the East Coast since records began in 1826, and the sweltering heat continued throughout the summer. Popular sentiments blamed the "freak weather" on nuclear bombs and perhaps also climate engineers, while meteorologists in a *New York Times* article rebutted the argument by saying that "even a moderate rainstorm [...] releases energy at a rate equivalent to several hundred atom bombs a minute." Instead, they blamed different natural factors but also "a small but definite increase in the past century in the percentage of carbon dioxide in the atmosphere" which has "heat-conserving properties similar to a greenhouse glass."[46] Polluting factories and deforestation were problems, and it may lead the Arctic ice caps to melt causing a worrying rise in ocean levels.

The greenhouse effect of carbon dioxide emissions was not only a concern of newspapers and popular journals catering chiefly to the politically liberal-leaning East Coast. *The Anniston Star* of southern Alabama, for example, had a lengthy article about the topic in July 1953. The past winter had been the second mildest in the state's history, followed by an abnormal spring with freak storms and more than 250 tornadoes, and then came the worst summer drought in decades. The public believed in a connection between "recent atom bomb blasts and the unusual atmospheric doings," but the meteorologists assured the readers that there was "absolutely no connection between the two." Instead, the weathermen argued that the freakish weather of 1953 was due to perfectly normal variations. But they were ready to agree with the layman that human agency also was to blame for a global warming weather trend. Greenland, for example, had "awakened from a frozen sleep to find itself an important cod fishing center and farmers in Scandinavian countries are now cultivating land which has lain under ice for 800 years." "Man's industrial activities and his destruction of vast forest areas has increased by three percent the amount of carbon dioxide in the atmosphere. [...] Nature's balance has been upset by the clearing of forested land, [and] [...] the polar ice caps have been melting steadily, producing an almost imperceptible rise in sea level."[47] A journalist in Indiana expressed a similar sentiment, blaming the warmer weather on natural events but also on "heat-retaining gases" that humans produce. Whatever

---

46 Leonard Engel, "The Weather Is Really Changing," *New York Times*, July 12, 1953, SM7. Cf. Gilbert N. Plass, "The Carbon Dioxide Theory of Climate Change," *Tellus* 8 (1956), 140–154.

47 Anonymous, "More about the Weather," *Anniston Star*, July 21, 1953, 4.

the cause of warmer weather, one point was clear: "You can't blame the atom bomb."[48]

Indeed, by the late 1950s, there were fewer people who believed that the bomb had an effect on the weather. The idea survived in the news mostly thanks to reporters pointing out that there was no such effect. One of its few late proponents of there being a connection between bombs and weather was Kimble, the climate engineer, who in an article in the *New York Times* in 1958 pointed out that the atmosphere was "as trigger-happy as some of us [...] as the heat released by exploding nuclear and thermonuclear devises [...] have observable effects on the equilibrium of the whole atmospheric system." Yet he too admitted that the bomb was probably not a major factor, as he gave credit to the alternative explanation that "the daily growing carbon dioxide content in the atmosphere" caused by the burning of fossil fuels could be an important reason for the global warming trend.[49] Other articles from the late 1950s covering climatic change do not mention nuclear weapons as a cause but tend instead to point to the emissions of carbon dioxide.[50]

The discovery of global warming is intrinsically linked to the detection of carbon dioxide emissions as a driver of climate change, a gas with an invisible impact of destructive change of similarity to the perception of radioactive clouds. To the lay reader of local newspapers, radioactive clouds and carbon dioxide gasses were alike, and the growing fair of the latter would build on the established fair of the first. Equally important is the gradual realization that humans could alter the atmosphere. This recognition of human atmospheric agency was propelled by lay people's belief that nuclear bombs can change the climate.

---

48 Anonymous, "Are Winters Getting Warmer?," *U.S. News and World Report* 36:2 (August 1, 1954), 37–39.

49 George H. T. Kimble, "Why the Weird Weather: Sun and Stars, Smoke and Bombs – All my Play a Part," *New York Times,* October 26, 1958, SM15.

50 James. S. DeLaurier, "Air Pollution One of Biggest Problems Facing America Today," (editorial), *Hammond Times*, November 5, 1957, 16. John Finney, "U. S. Is Urged to Seek Methods To Control the World's Weather," *The New York Times*, January 1, 1958, 1. Anonymous, "World Scientists Plan Study of Oceans for Clues to Climate," *Yuma Sun*, October 4, 1958, 15. Anonymous, "A Warmer Earth Evident at Poles," *New York Times*, February 15, 1959, 112. Anonymous, "Austrian Alps Glaziers Melt at Record Rate," *Berkshire Eagle*, April 9, 1959, 21.

CONCLUSION

For the Love of Bombs

"Canned Curandero" was an "uncorked love bomb" the Occult Society in San Antonio, Texas, used in the 1960s to get in the groove.[1] They sprayed themselves with lysergic acid diethylamide (LSD) on a can so that they could enter into a merry kind of reality. Similarly, historians of physics have been spraying their work with evidence from the "canned curandero" of the *Smyth Report*, creating a merry historical realm for U.S. audiences uncomfortable with the ugly realities of atomic weaponry. The norm in this historiography has been to replicate the report to create an escape from the horrid truths about nuclear bombs. The Oscar-winning *Oppenheimer* film (2023) may serve as a telling example of such opium of the people. There are honorable exceptions, of course, but the rule of thumb has been to frame the history of the making of the bomb as stories of brilliant (but also tormented) physicists. All histories are mediations on current affairs, which raises the question of why this narrative of dazzling scientific bomb makers still prevails. For the U.S. audience, it's a comfortable narrative of technological, scientific, and moral superiority masking the horrific environmental and social truths of atomic bombs. For the love of bombs, it's time to forget these scientists and face the ugly historical realities of nuclear weapons.

To enter that reality, one has to take the bull by the horns and come to terms with Hiroshima and Nagasaki. One has to be willing to see lay victims in the eye, as forcefully done by John Hersey in his famous report from 1946 and later by numerous authors, documentary makers, and artists. Moreover, one has to investigate the damaging impact the bomb had on U.S. environments, cultures, societies, people (including the "downwinders"), and scientific communities. This book has been an attempt to move beyond official histories and address the horrid realities of how the bomb was made and the damaging impact that had in America and beyond. In doing so, I have taken the cue from Hersey in focusing on the lives of ordinary people, and not highbrow scientists.

---

1 Sam Kindrick, "Occult Society is Getting Canny," *San Antonio Express,* May 4, 1967, 17B.

The material history of how the bomb was made does not begin with advanced equations on the blackboard in some highbrow laboratory but in a dirty mine in the Dene First Nation in northern Canada. It was here the uranium began its path of pain. It was dug up and handled with the bare hands of blue-collar miners, many of whom were indigenous. Their work and suffering from subsequent cancers represent the origin of the trail of nuclear suffering that the bomb created. The first warnings against the destructive impact of the bomb did not come from some highbrow thinker, but in a dark indigenous prophesy of the 1880s, long before anyone imagined the destructive power of uranium.

Following the material history, the next stop in the uranium's path of pain was the Wheat community whose name and existence have largely been forgotten even by savvy historians of the bomb. The destruction of Wheat and its environment enabled the creation of the ecological disaster zone named Oak Ridge after the war. Wheat was a closely knit community of people caring for each other and the land, while what became Oak Ridge nurtured a culture of dispersed individualism disconnected from the environment in which they worked. The people who colonized the land of Wheat enriched uranium that caused a trail of lasting damage to local environments before it was assembled into bombs that were subsequently dropped on Hiroshima and Nagasaki, causing unspeakable horrors.

Most laypeople in the United States had a festive reaction to the events in Japan that reflected an end to a war that was also gruesome to Allied soldiers. The *Smyth Report* was issued in the context of these celebrations, focusing on the intellectual achievements of the nuclear science community. What is remarkable, is that this festive national mood concerning nuclear destruction would continue for decades as a marker of scientific and cultural superiority. One telling articulation of this culture was the frequent comparison of (an)atomical women to bombs, as in the "bombshell" and "sex bombs" metaphors that were used well into the late 1950s and beyond.

The use of nuclear arsenal to frame cultural debates was far-reaching and well beyond what's covered in this book. Indeed, atomic weaponry would inspire designs of homes, furniture, cars, and various everyday objects creating, in effect, a cultural militarism for ordinary people.[2] Highbrow academics were no better. The following examples could be subject to further research: the ecologist Rachel Carson famously framed her argument against dichloro-diphenyl-trichloroethane (DDT) in *Silent Spring* (1962) as that of an invisible

---

2 Charrissa Terranova, *Automotive Prosthetic* (Austin: University of Texas Press, 2014), 187–226.

radioactive fallout.[3] Michael W. Sterns, the Commissioner at the Bureau of Reclamation, framed human population growth as "The Population Bomb!" in 1955, an expression the biologist Paul R. Ehrlich made famous in his book with the same title from 1968.[4] In his follow-up, *The Race Bomb* (1977), Ehrlich would depict racism as a destructive nuclear weapon. On the other end of the political spectrum, the activist James Farrell's infamous *Give Us Your Poor: The Immigration Bomb* (1975) may serve as an example of how the political right thought of immigrants as being as damaging to the nation as that of a nuclear blast.[5] And the list goes on. Indeed, it's hard to think of debates in American culture that have not been framed as a nuclear weapon.

Further investigations of the bomb metaphor could discuss the people's history of the "theoretical bomb," the Christian "biblical bomb," the alternative "spiritual bomb," the romantic "poetry bomb," the film thrill of the "time bomb," the political "T-bomb (truth bomb)," the diplomatic efforts behind a "peace bomb," and so forth. Not to mention the fear and trembling associated with the "calorie bomb," the "peanut butter bomb," and the "chocolate bomb." The nuclear weapon has, perhaps, been the most important allegory in post-war U.S. social debate and popular culture. Yet it's still bewildering that the horrors of Hiroshima could ever emerge as a metaphor for pigging out on chocolate. Or that the emotional impact of a bikini-dressed "sex bomb" can be compared to that of ground zero in Nagasaki. Ordinary citizens would live in denial about the horrors of the bomb thanks to these masks. Let's therefore, state the obvious: *the bomb is not a metaphor.* These expressions stand in the way of recognizing its destructive power and the possibility of an atomic apocalypse.

These images also stand in the way of recognizing that the horrors of Hiroshima not only continued in Nagasaki but also on the atolls in the Pacific Ocean and beyond. More than a hundred bombs were used by the United States to annihilate the ecological and human communities on these atolls, and the majority of these bombs were much more powerful than those dropped on the Japanese cities. (Pause for reflection). It's about time the United States—along with the Russians, French, Chinese, and British—come to terms with their colonialism by letting the story of destruction be at the core of the narrative

---

3 Ralph H. Lutts, "Chemical Fallout: Rachel Carson's Silent Spring, Radioactive Fallout, and the Environmental Movement," *Environmental Review* 9 (1985), 210–225.

4 Michael W. Straus, *Why Not Survive?* (New York: Simon and Schuster, 1955), 15–28. Paul R. Ehrlich, *The Population Bomb* (New York: Ballentine, 1968).

5 Paul R. Ehrlich and S. Shirley Feldman, *The Race Bomb* (New York: Quandrangle, 1977). James Ferrell, *Give us Your Poor: The Immigration Bomb* (San Francisco: Fulton-Hall, 1975).

of how the bomb was continuously *enhanced*, as "the making" of the bomb did not stop in the Los Alamos Laboratory. The scientific research continued for decades. Indeed, it continues today.

Although this book is a contribution to a "people's history" of how the bomb was made, it's important not to dismiss the work of highbrow scientists. Thanks to their hard work that we know what's causing global warming. At the same time, this book has documented the importance of ordinary citizens in enabling the same scientists to be heard in the larger press. The larger public had the silent destructive agent of radioactive clouds in mind when they learned about the emission of carbon dioxide from the burning of fossil fuels as a cause of climatic change. Climate scientists were called upon to answer lay citizens' concerns about radioactive clouds and the warming power of nuclear bombs to the atmosphere. The uneducated public may have something important to say in scientific considerations, as it was their fear about the bombs' impact on the weather that made possible the wider acceptance of anthropogenic climate change.

As this book comes to a close, there is a final key question to consider: "What if the target for the bomb had been an American City?"[6] First raised by the U.S. administration in 1946, it's a question contemplated by all parties ever since. The government's answer was to send the country into a frenzy of infrastructural projects meant to protect the nation, from evacuation highways and massive military bunkers to tiny shelters dug down on the nuclear family's front lawn. Perhaps the indigenous uranium handlers visited at the beginning of this book can help us not to lose eyesight of what a nuclear attack on an American city would most likely entail. The predictions of the Sahtu Got'ine's medicine man, Louis Ayah, remain eerily relevant, as in the case of his prophecy of how the world will end. It will resemble that of a swift nuclear Armageddon: "This is how fast it will end. Clap your hands together in front of you as fast as you can, it will be faster than that."[7]

---

6 Franklin D'Olier, et al., *The Effects of Atomic Bombs on Hiroshima and Nagasaki* (Washington: Government Printing Office, 1946), 36.

7 Louis Ayah, "The Prophecy's of Louis Ayah," *The People*, 2016. Prophecy 7. Undated, 1930s or earlier.

ACKNOWLEDGMENTS

This book could not have been written without the ongoing support and encouragement of Jimena Canales. Although we may not agree on everything herein, we have shared an interest in the urgent need to retell the history of how atomic bombs were made. I have also benefitted a great deal from presenting the material to students in my course History of Environmental Sciences at the Gallatin School of Individualized Study at New York University. My colleagues at the New York City History of Science Working Group and New York University have also offered constructive feedback and support, particularly Eugene Cittadino, Karen Holmberg, Mitchell Joachim, and Matthew Stanly. Along the way, I have also enjoyed comments from Debora R. Coen, Camila Canales, Per Högselius, Charissa N. Terranova, Catherine Townsend, and Spencer R. Weart. My gratitude also goes to *JAMIT* where the first chapter was previously published. Moreover, The Gallatin School's Dean, Victoria Rosner, has liberally supported the project with an award from the Gallatin Publications Subvention Fund. Lastly, it's been a joy working with my editorial team at Anthem Press who facilitated helpful anonymous reviewers. My gratitude goes out to all of you.

INDEX